Floral
Alphabet
Coloring Book

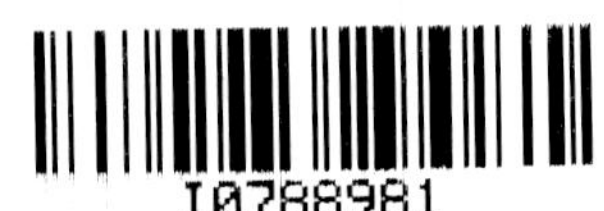

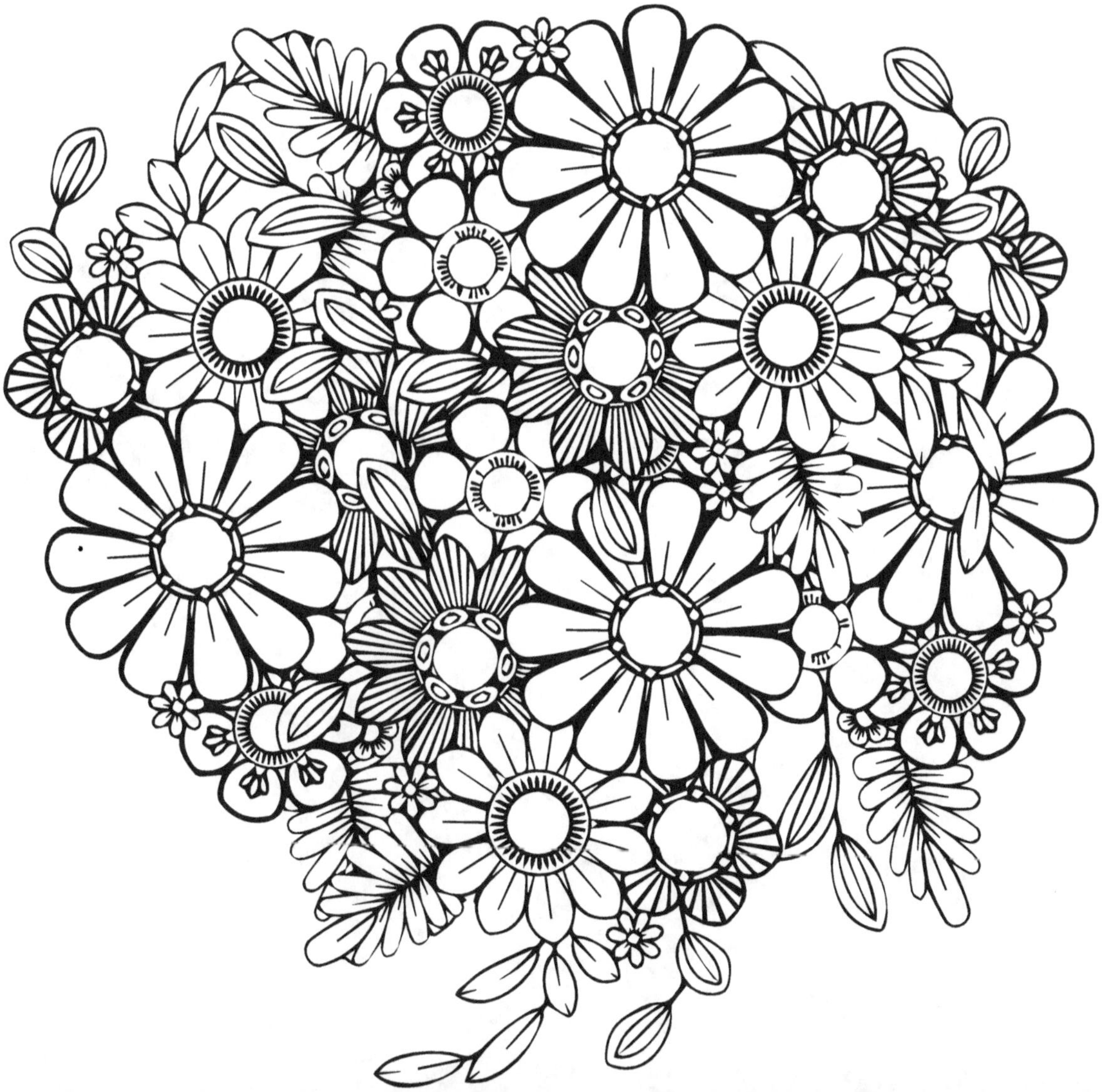

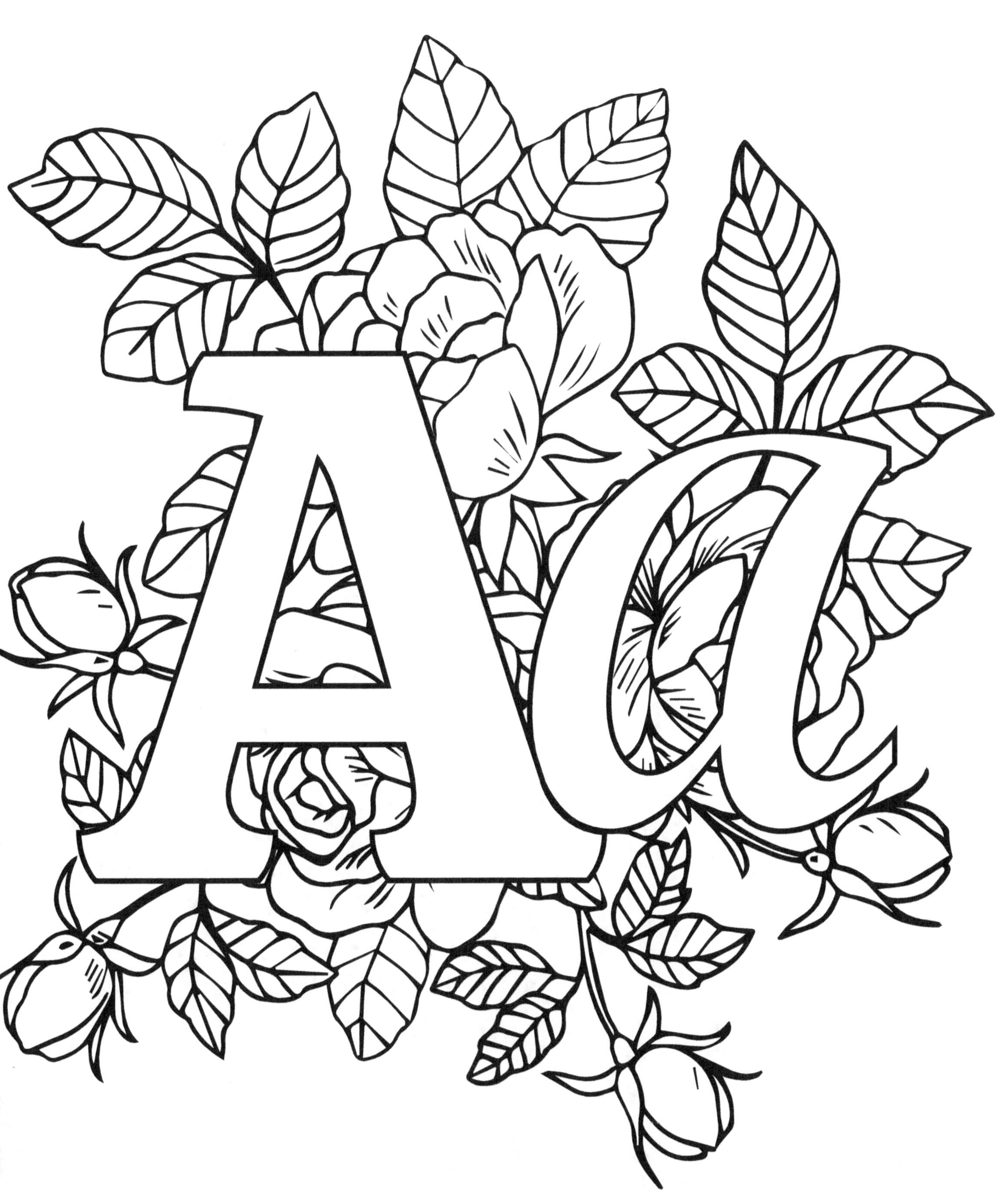

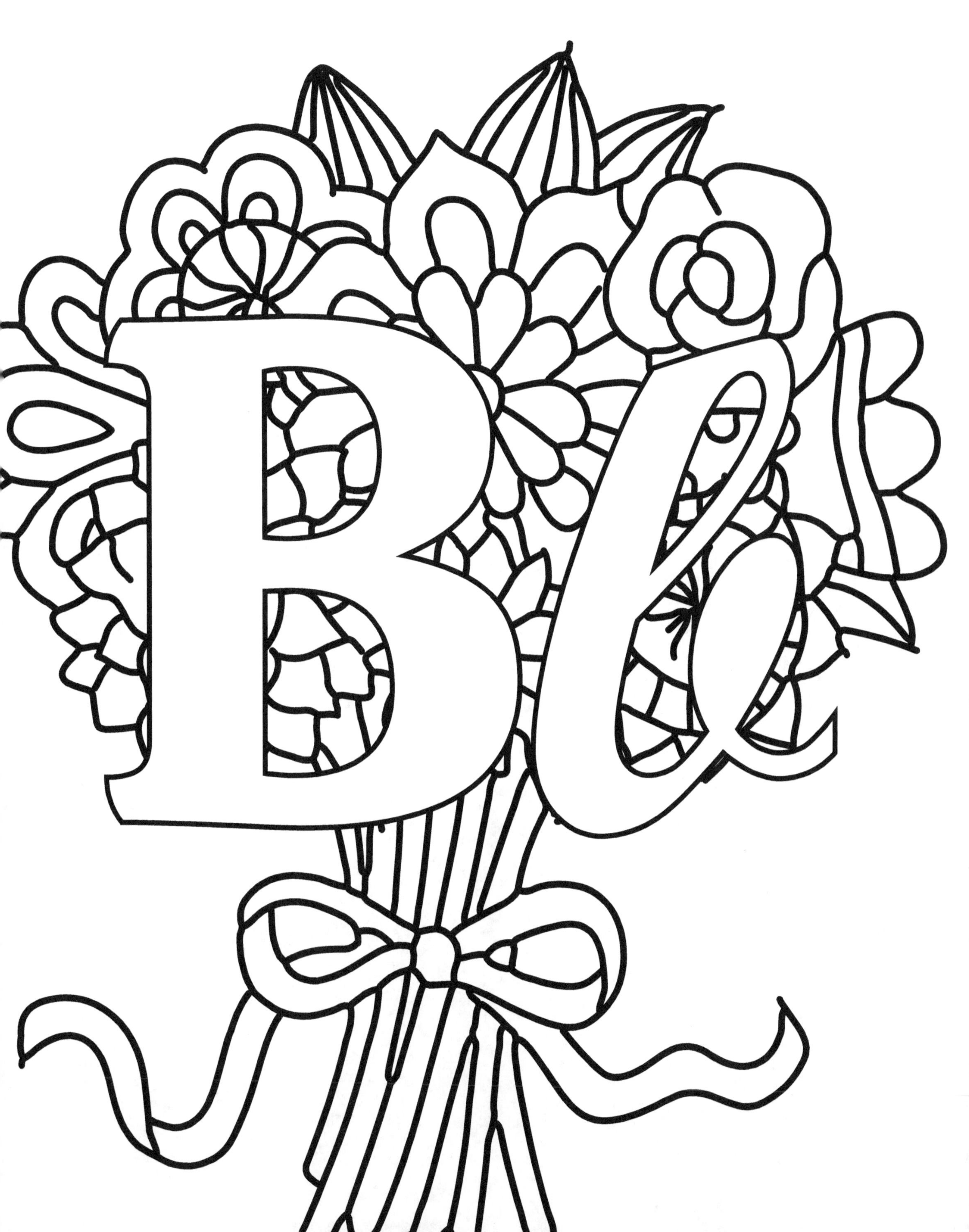

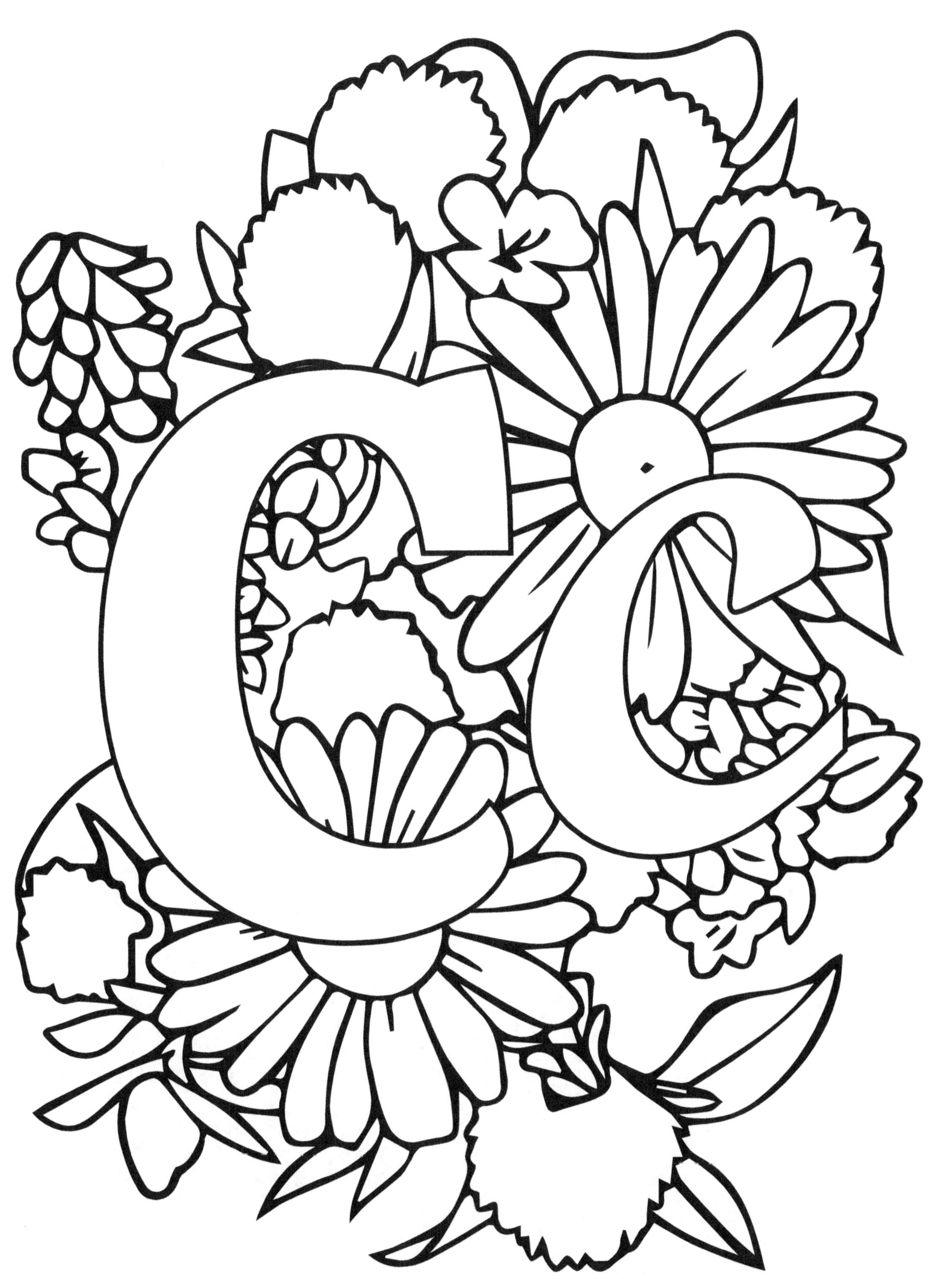

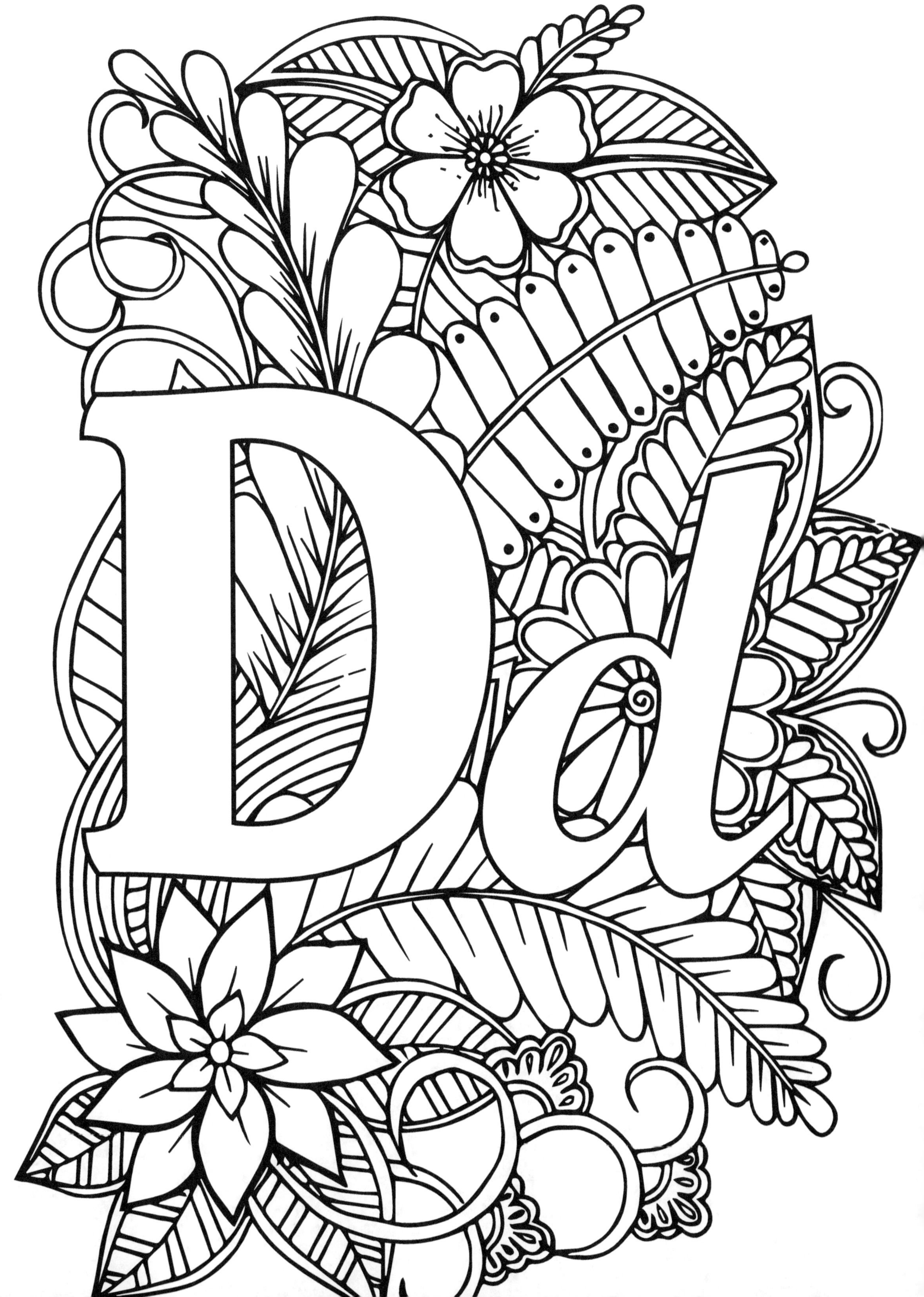

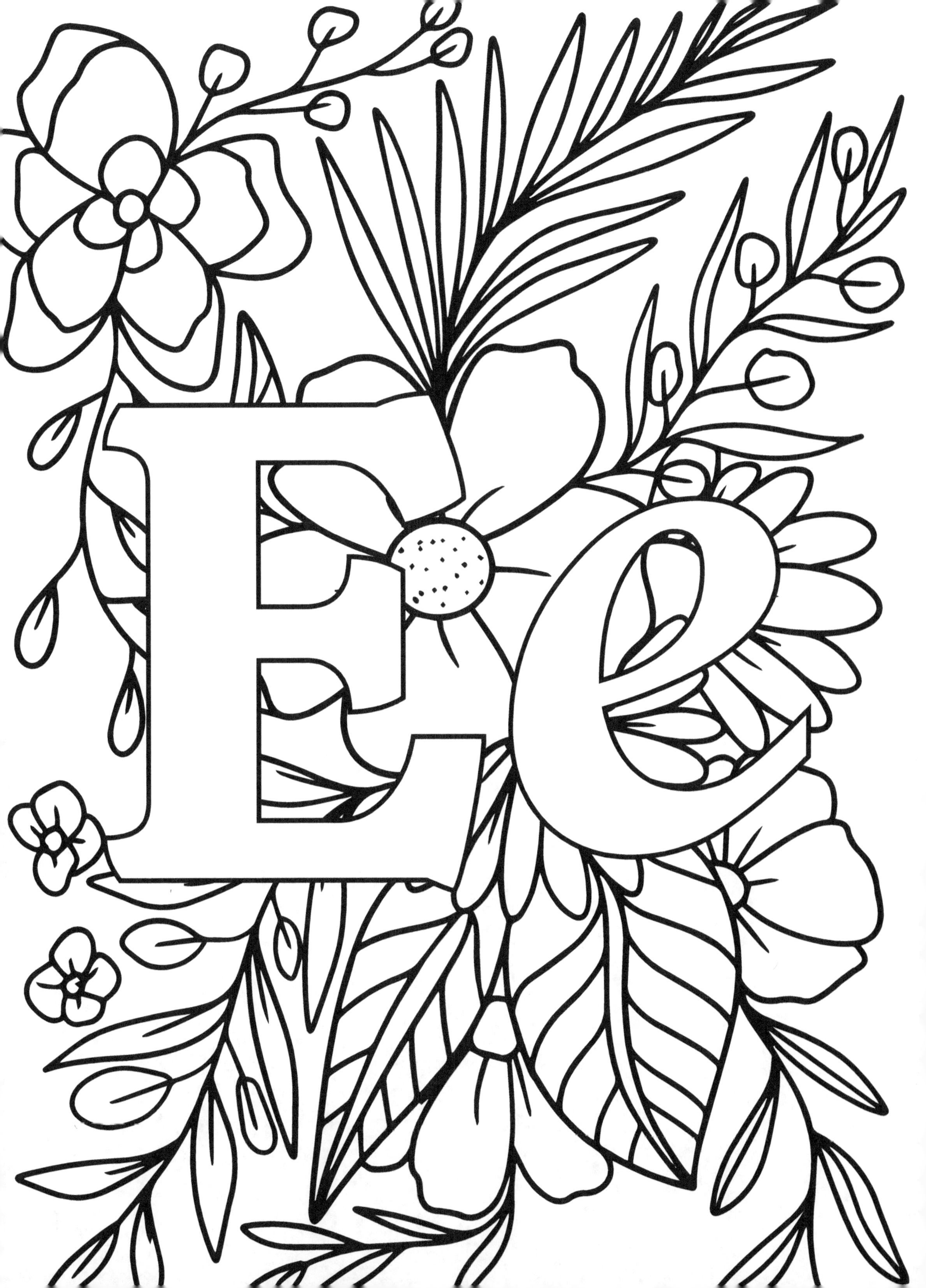
Ee

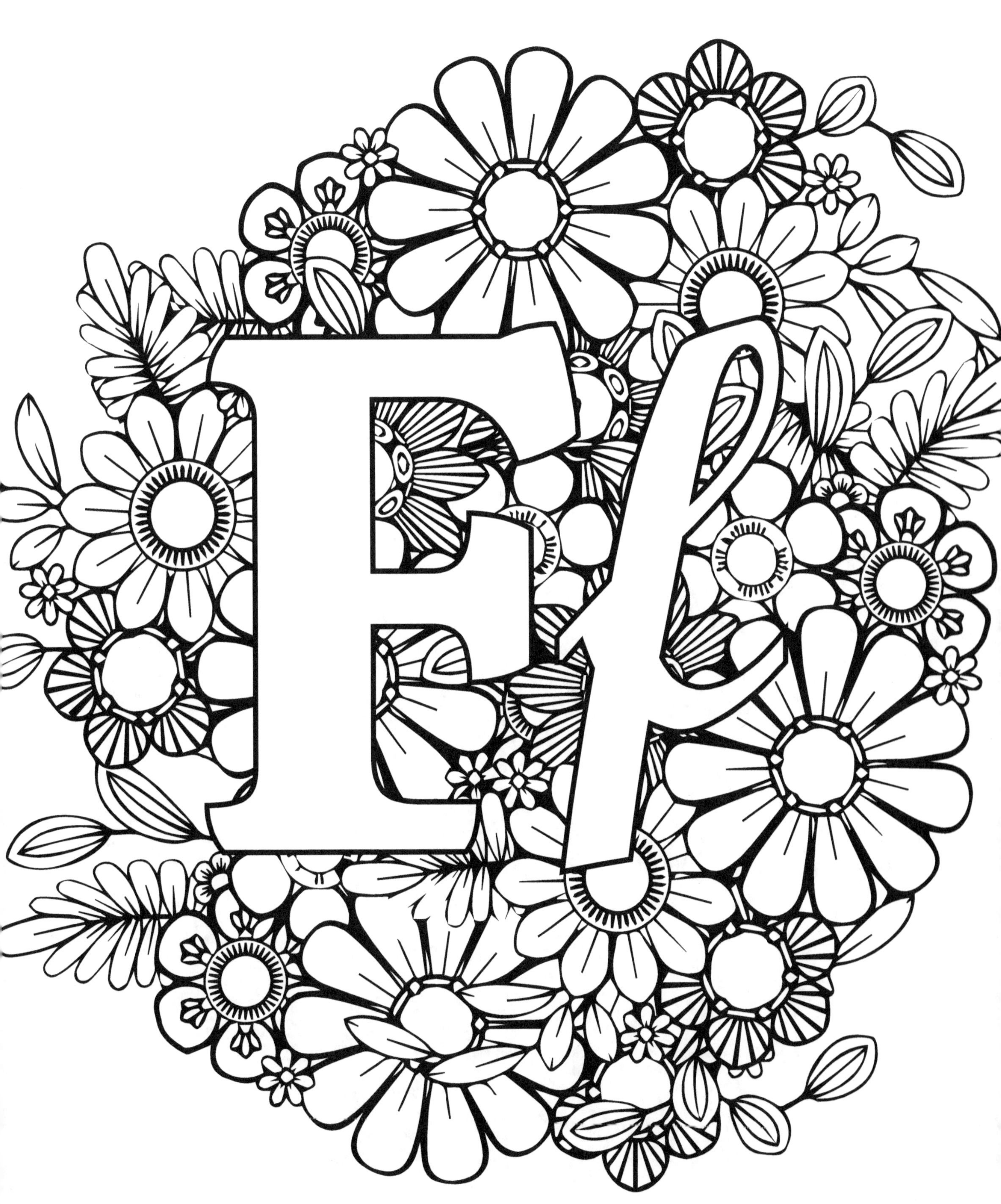

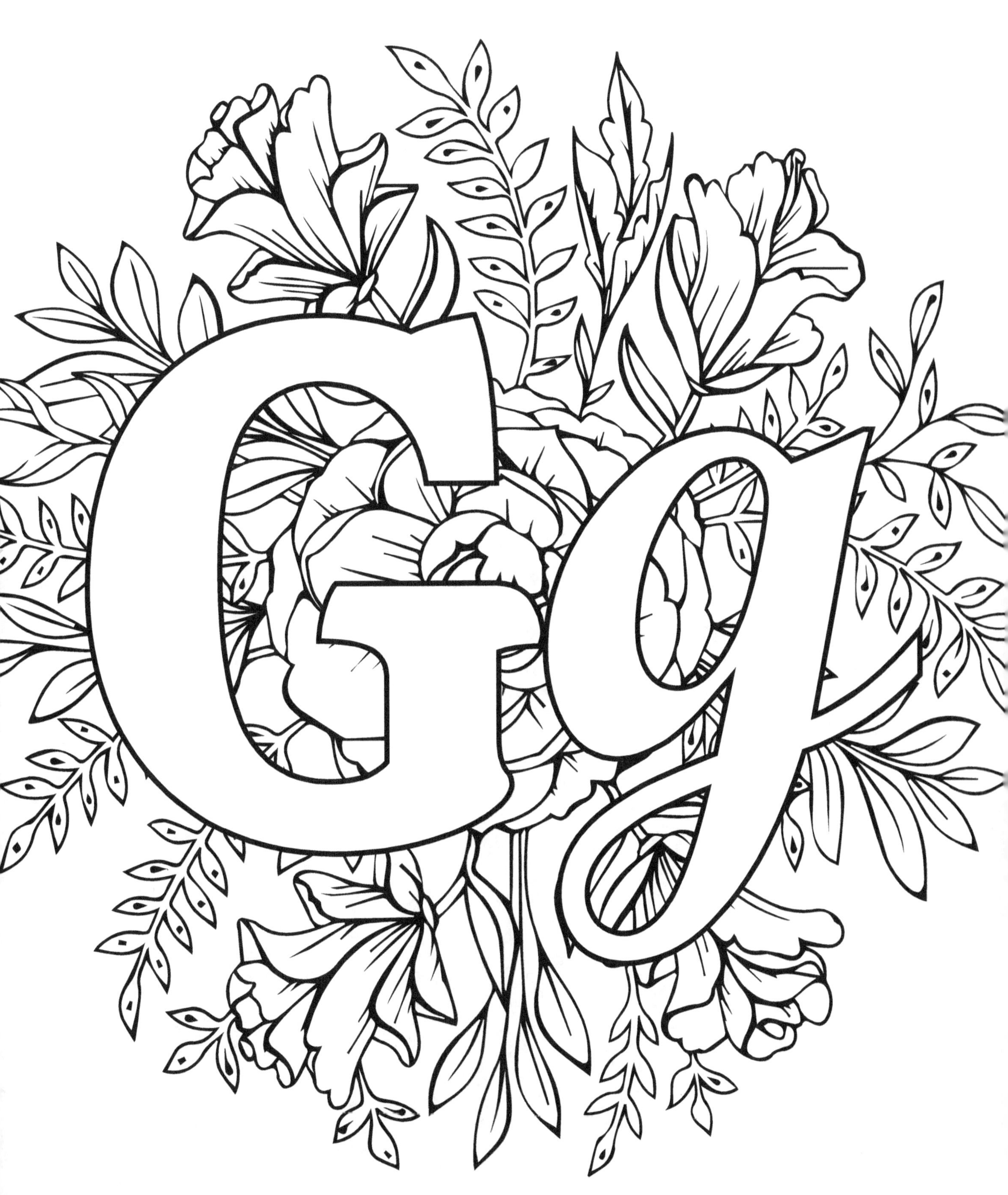

Gg

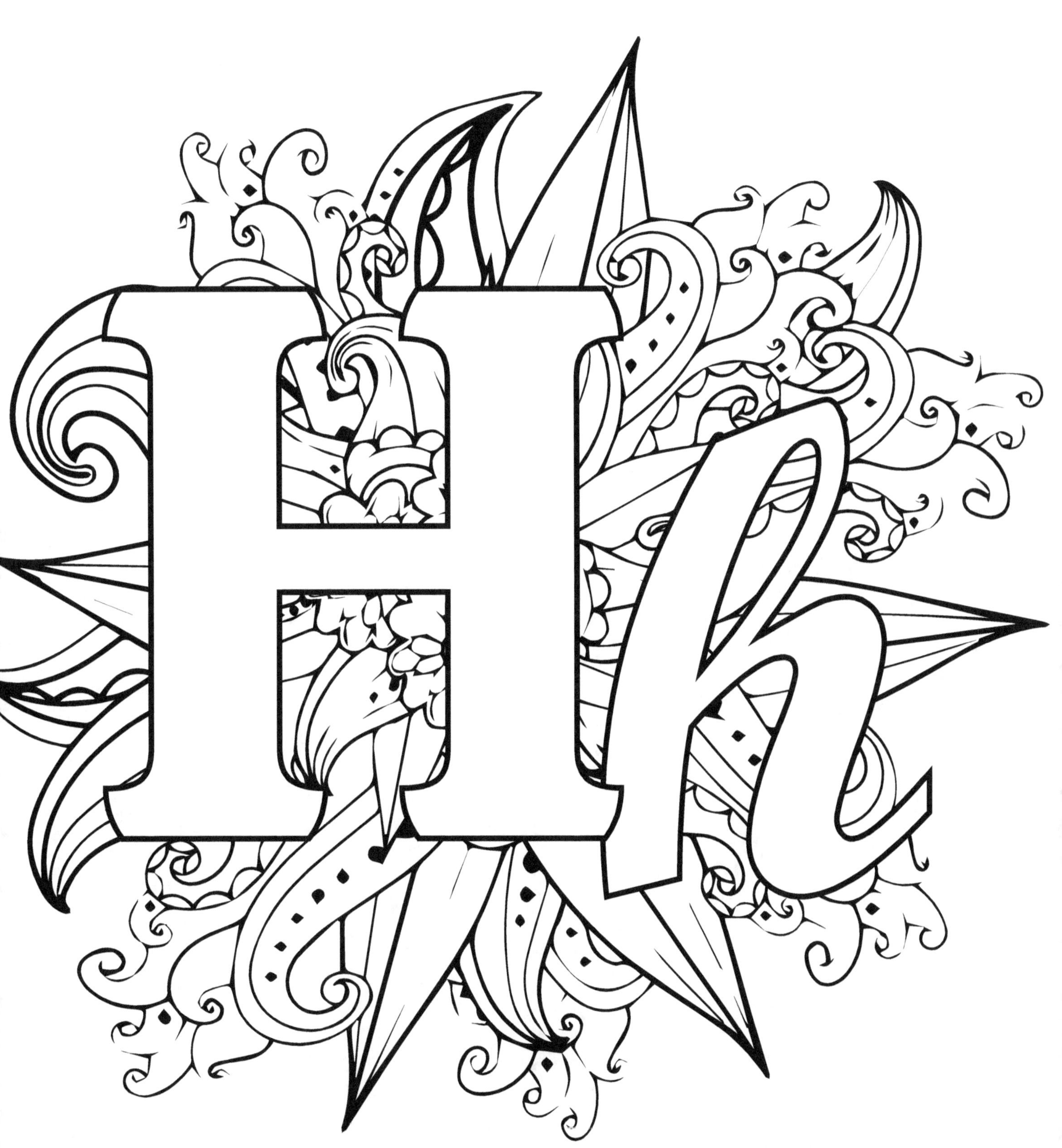

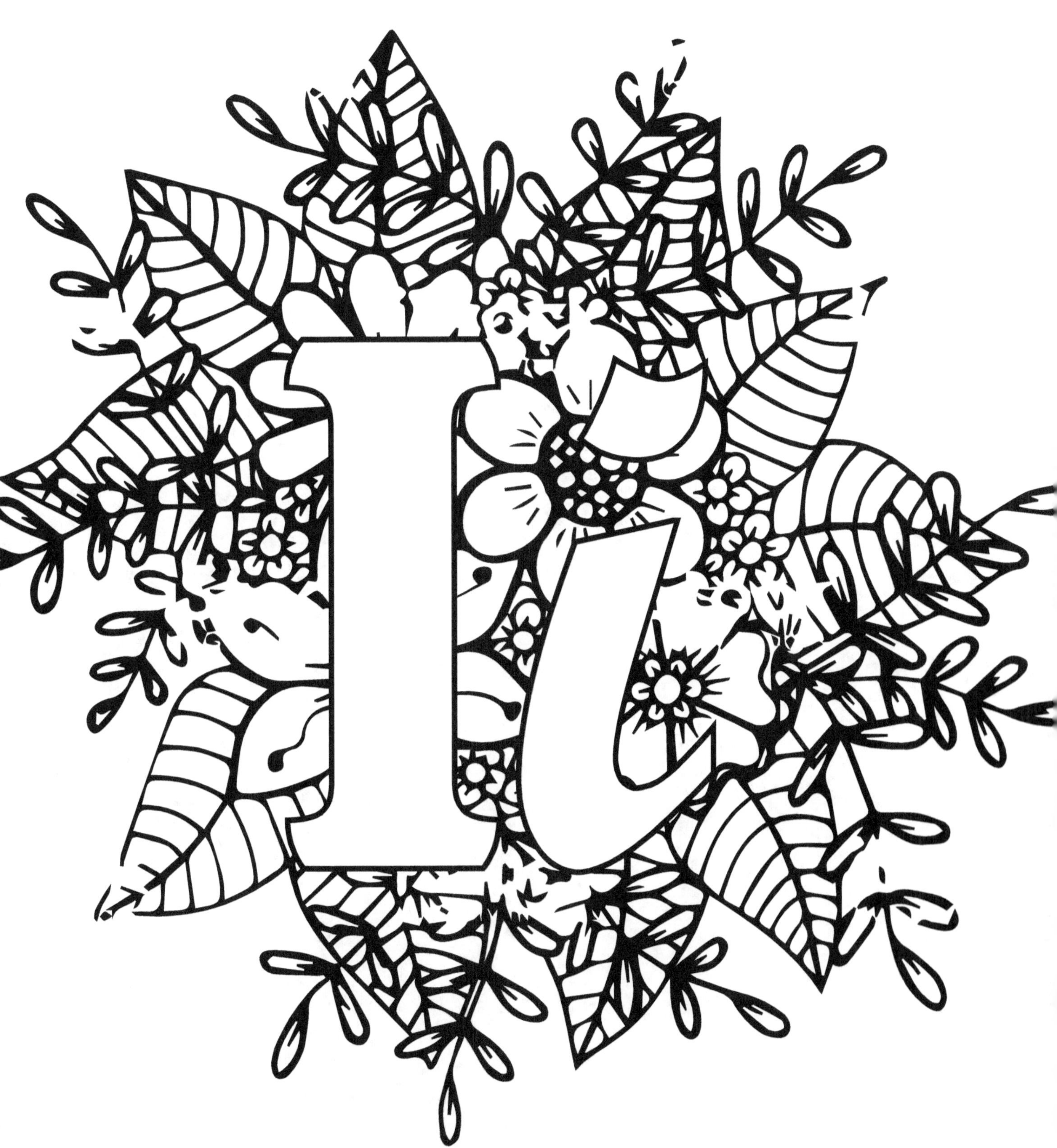

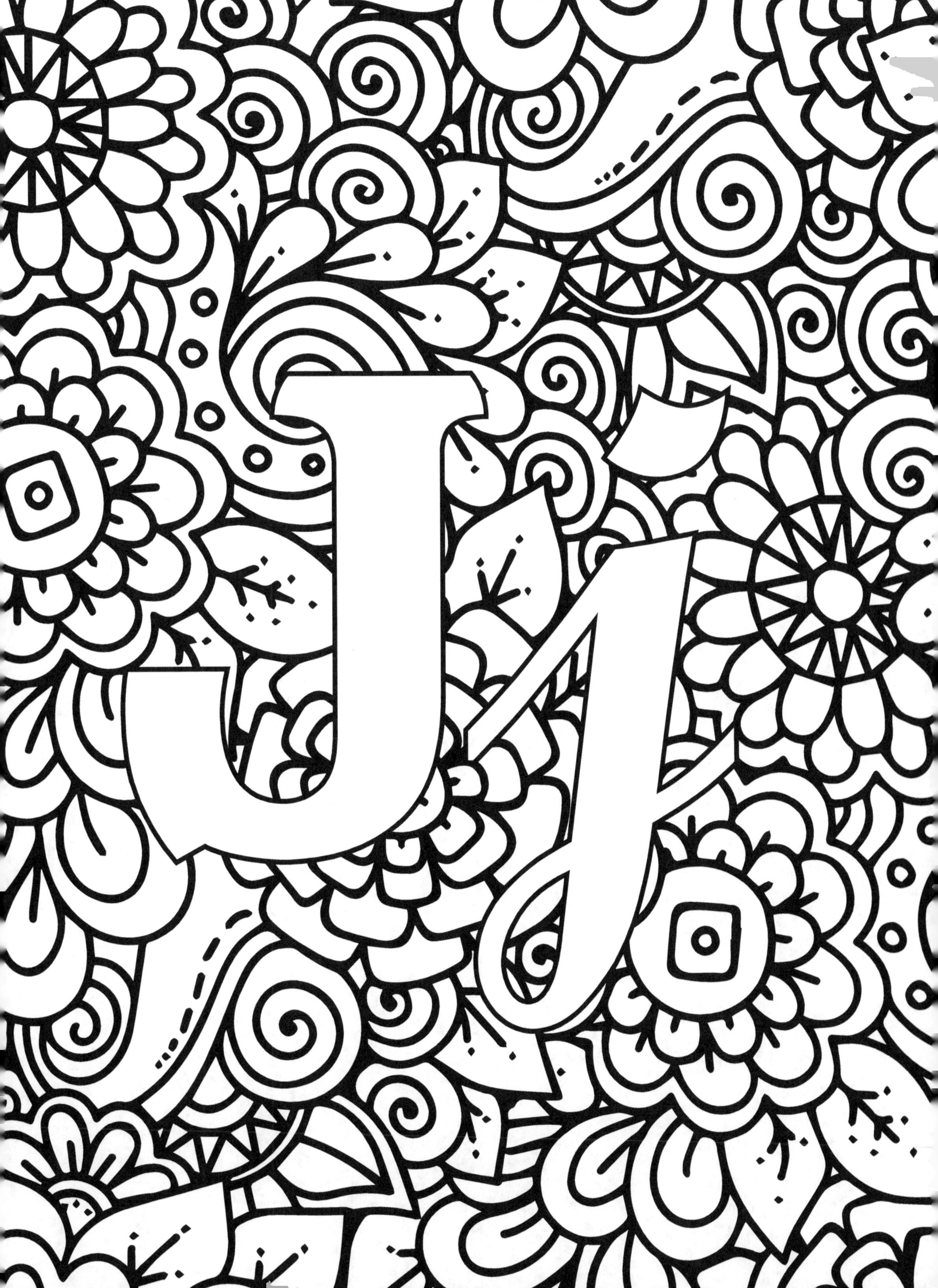

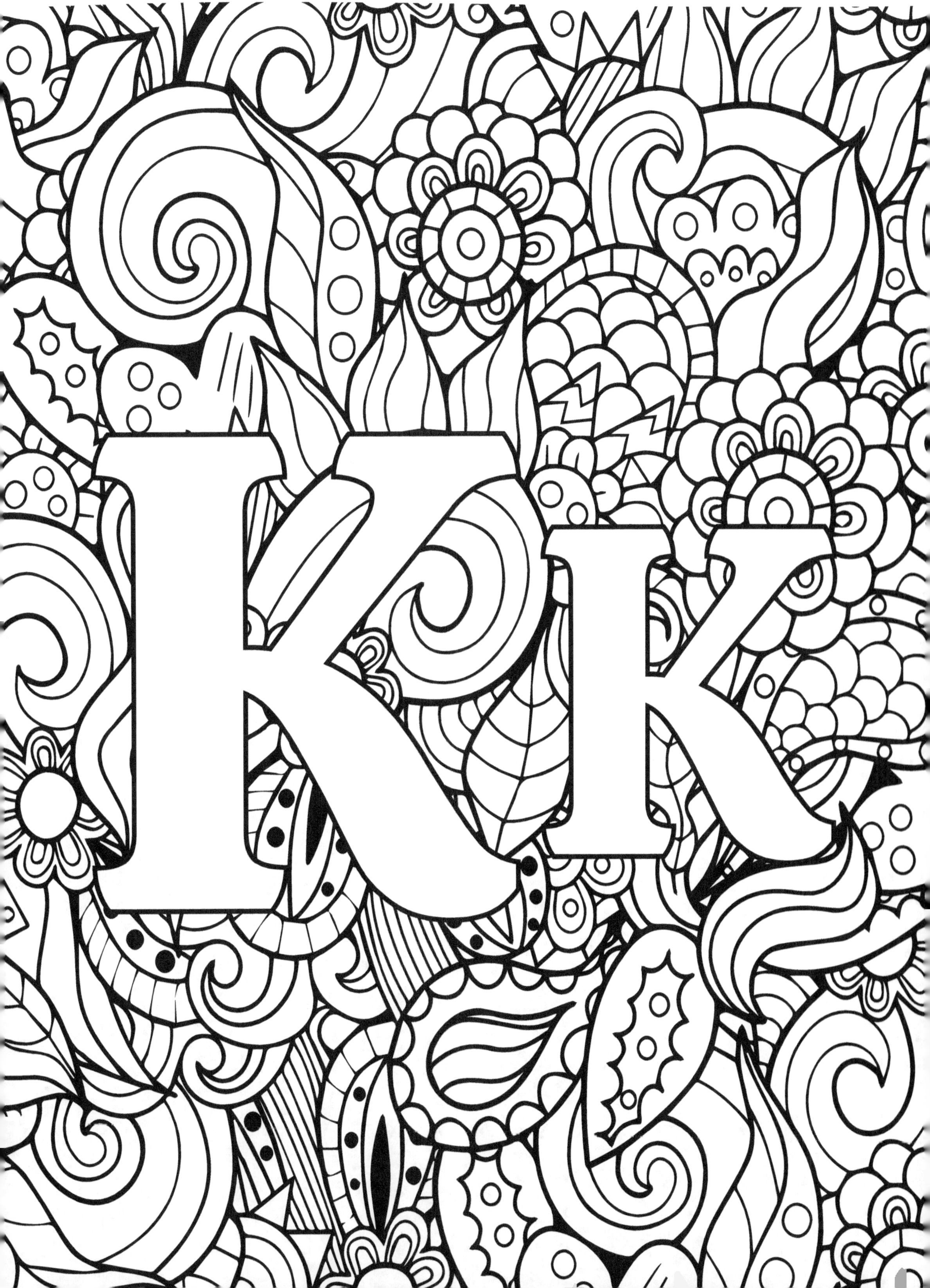

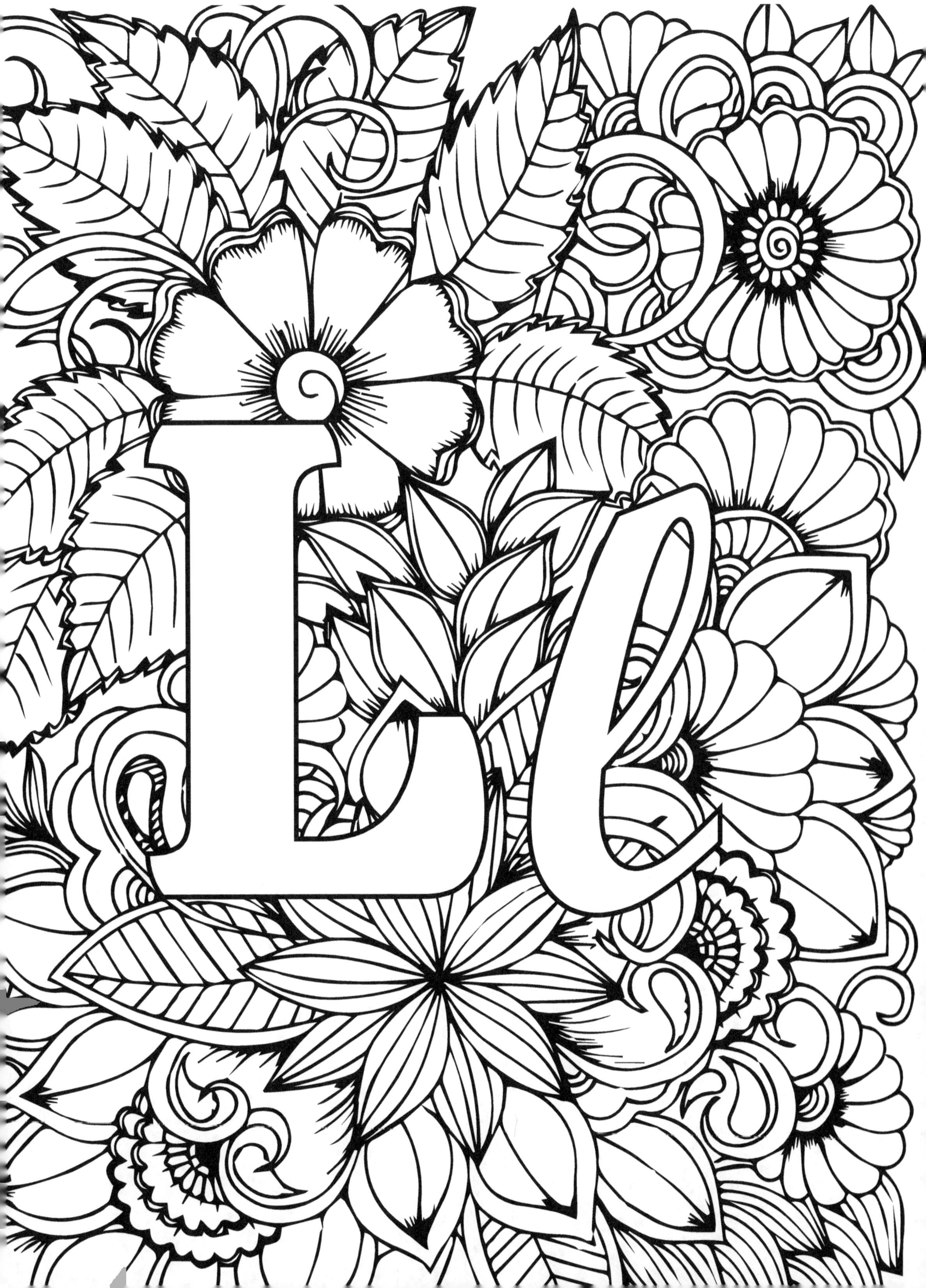

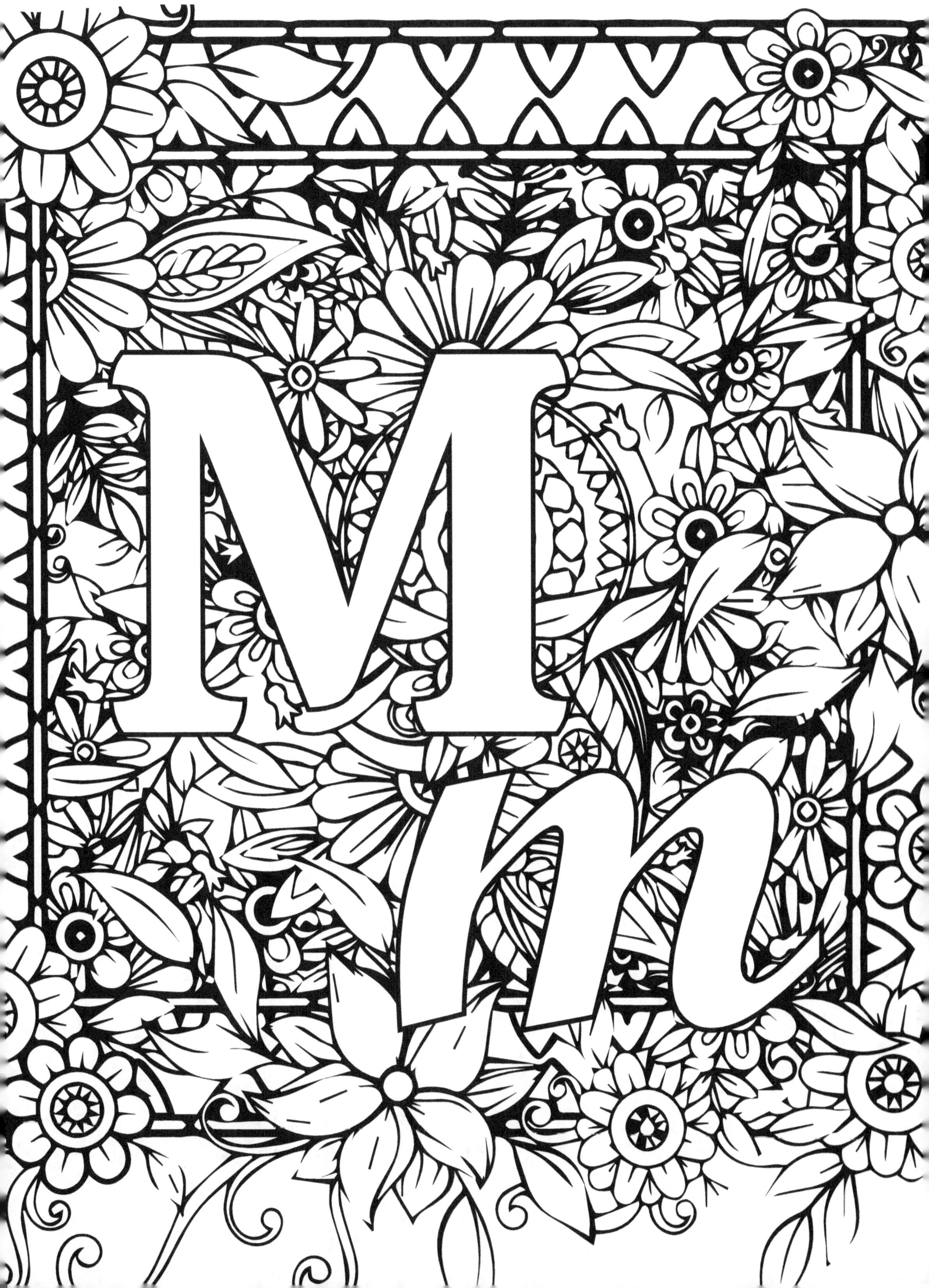
M
m

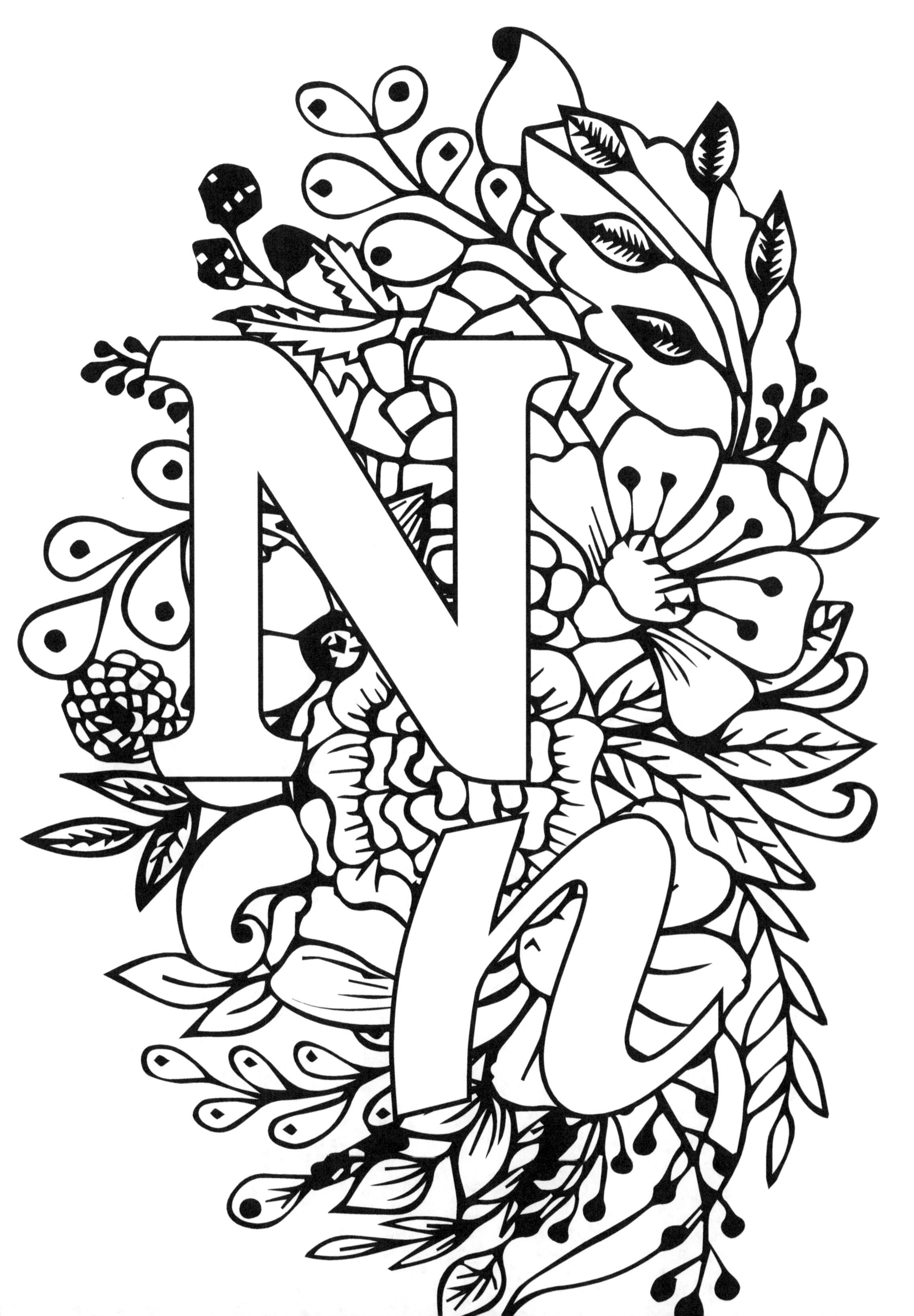

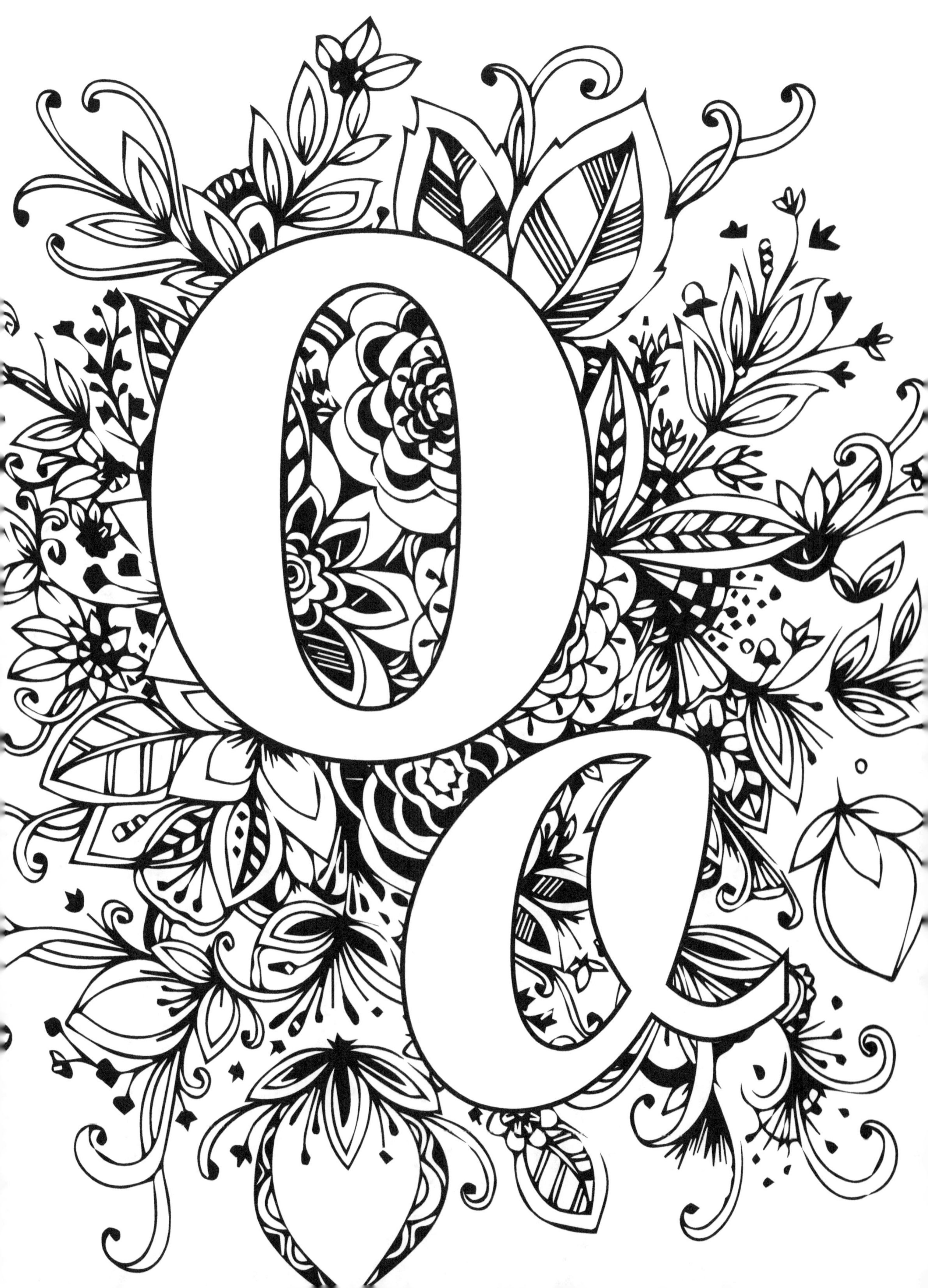

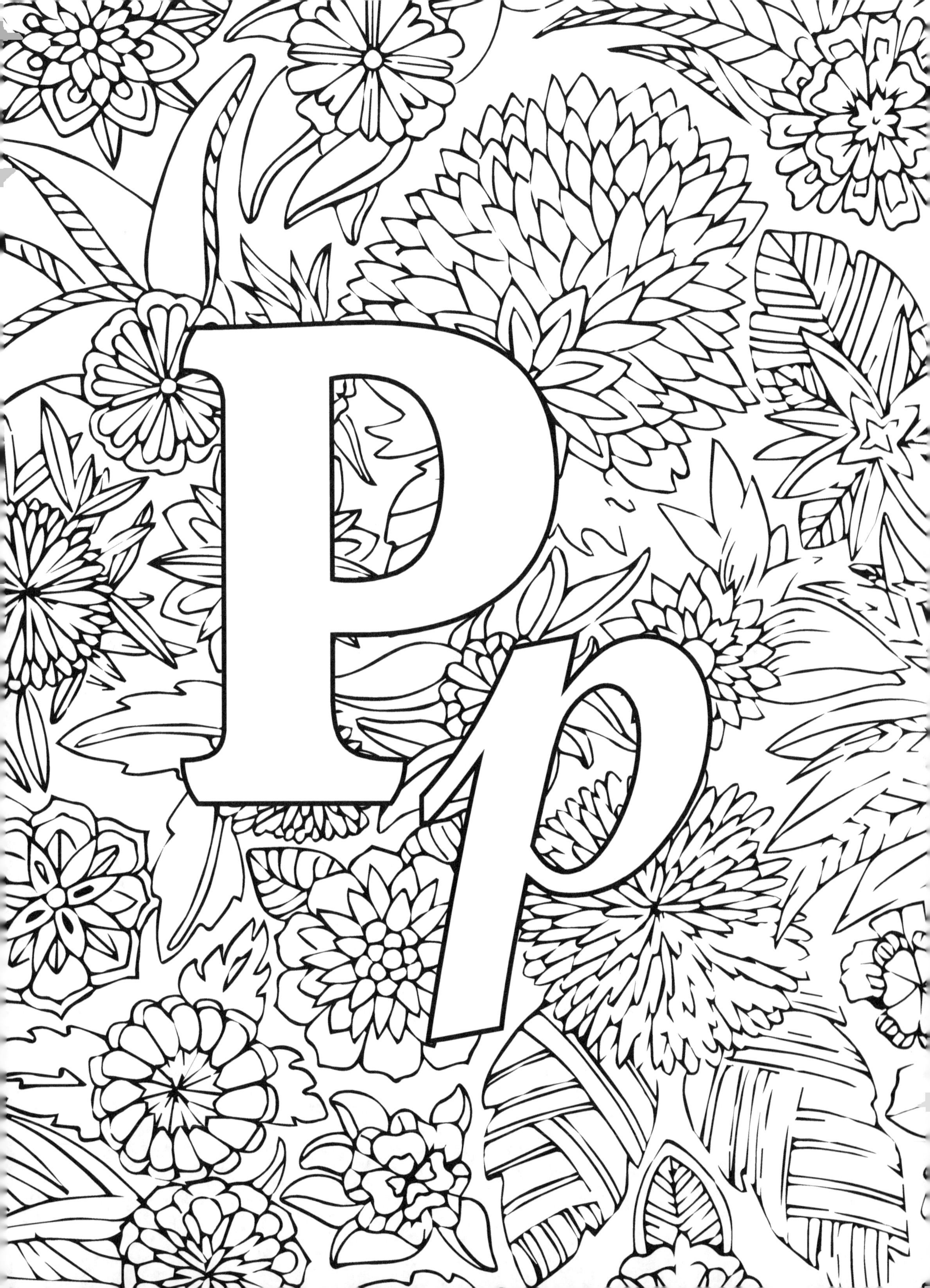

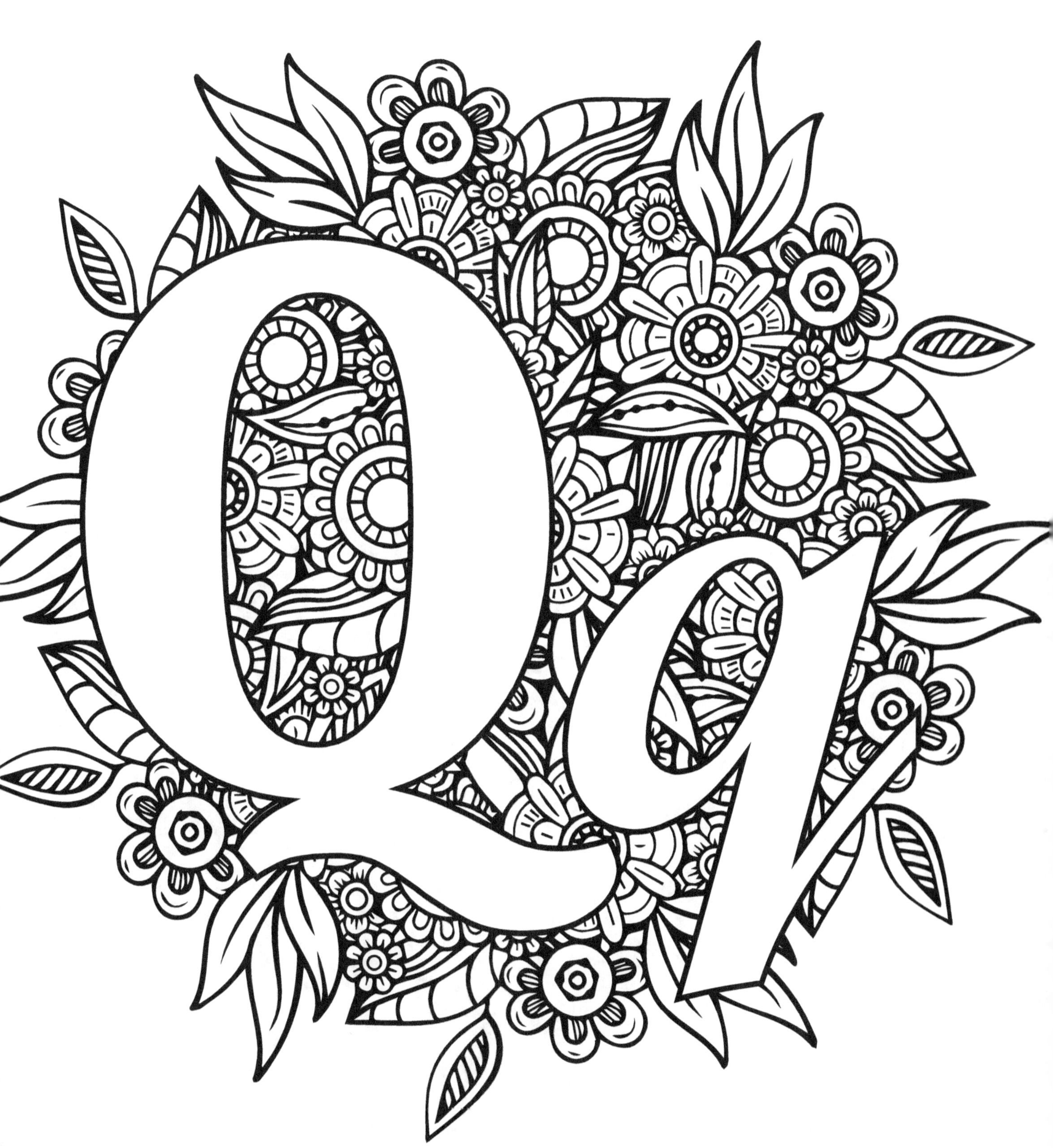

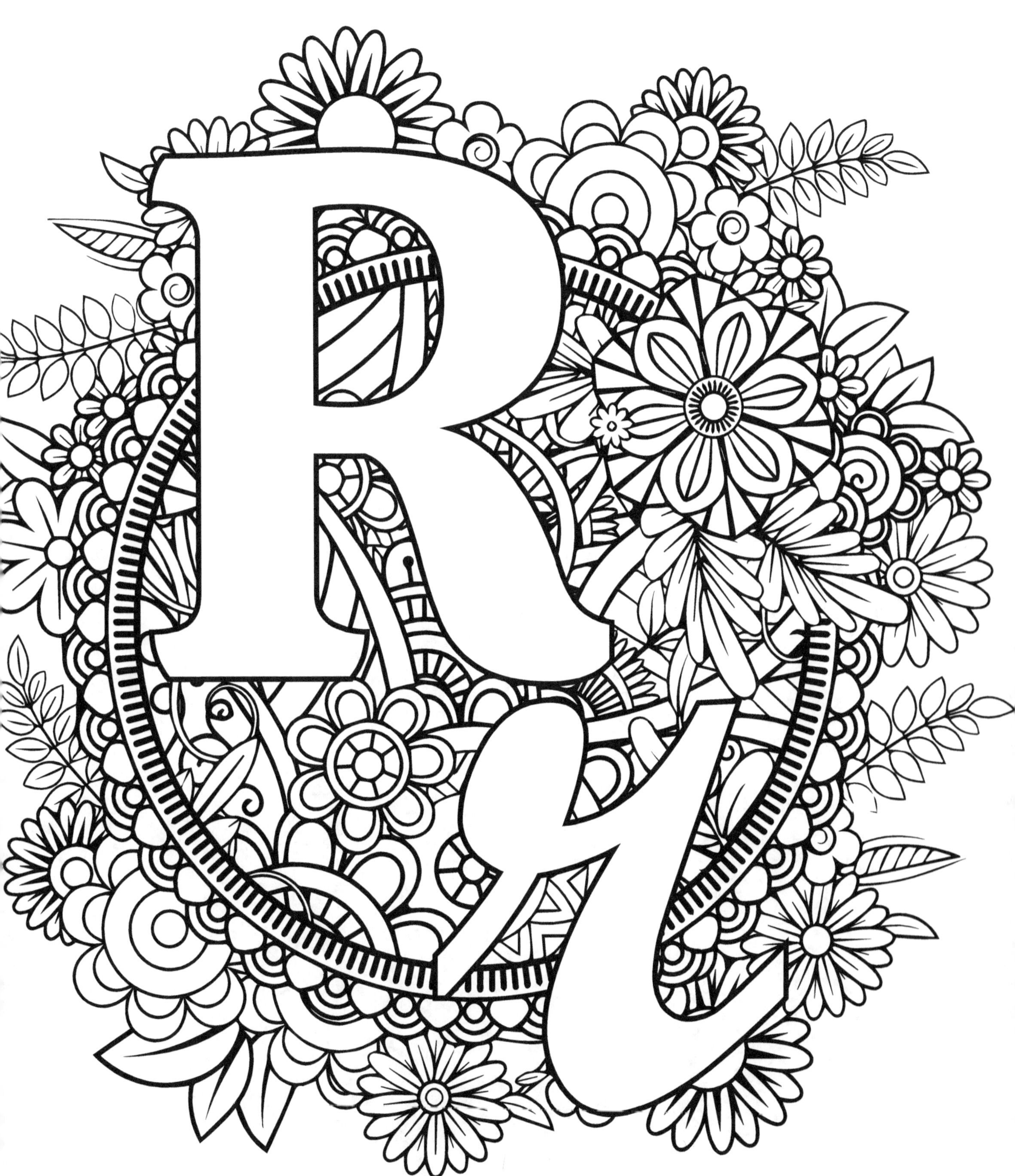

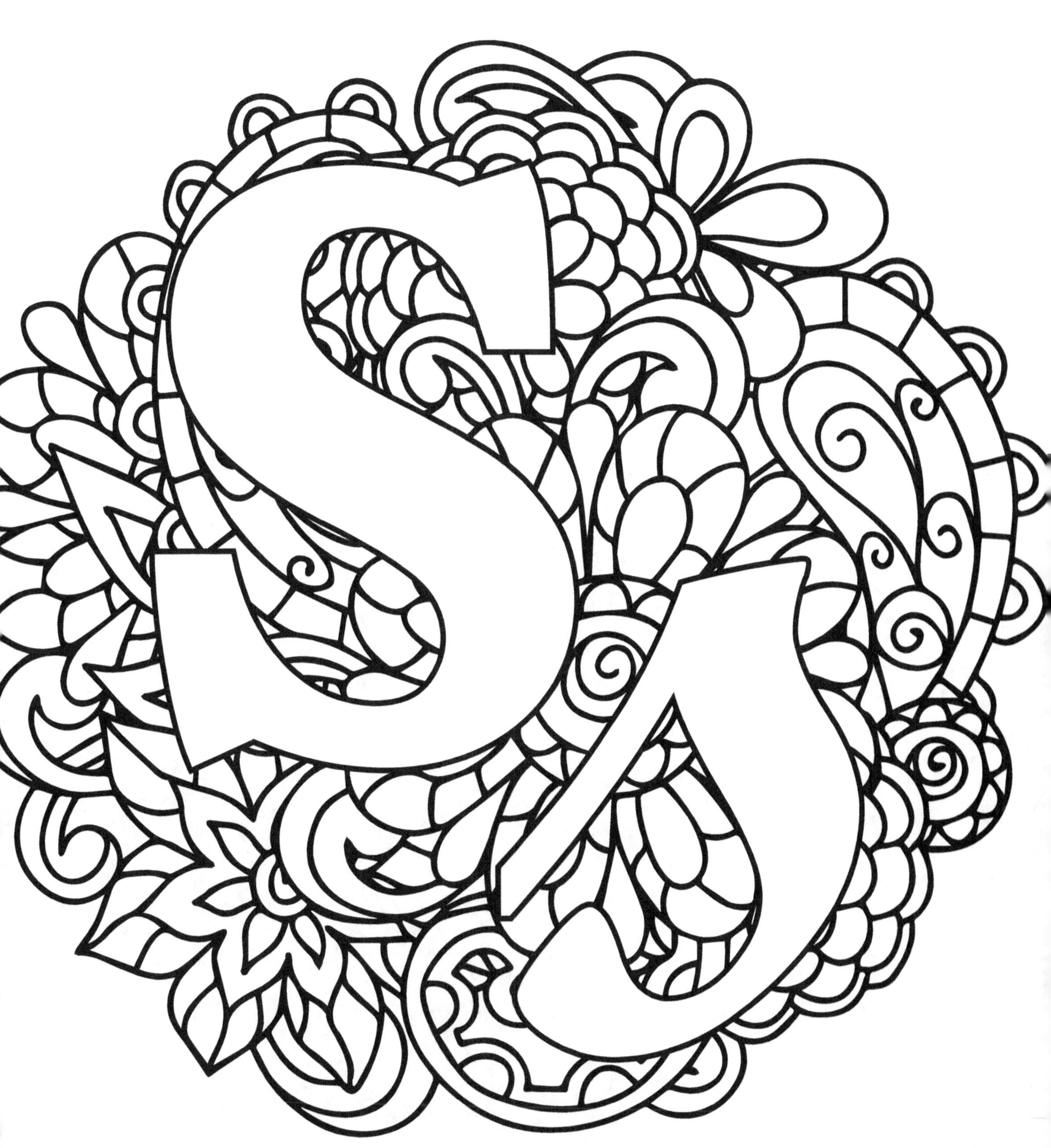

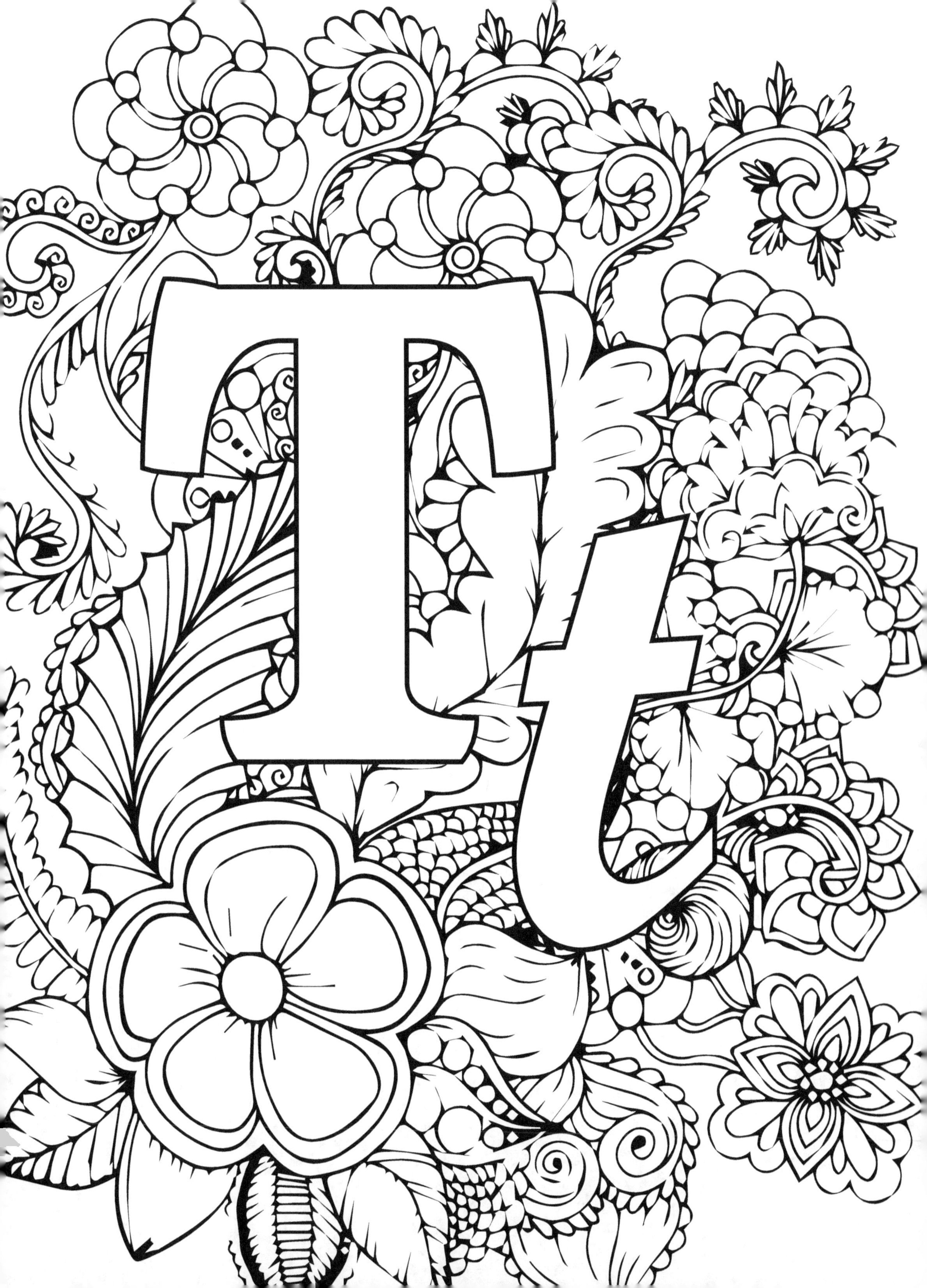

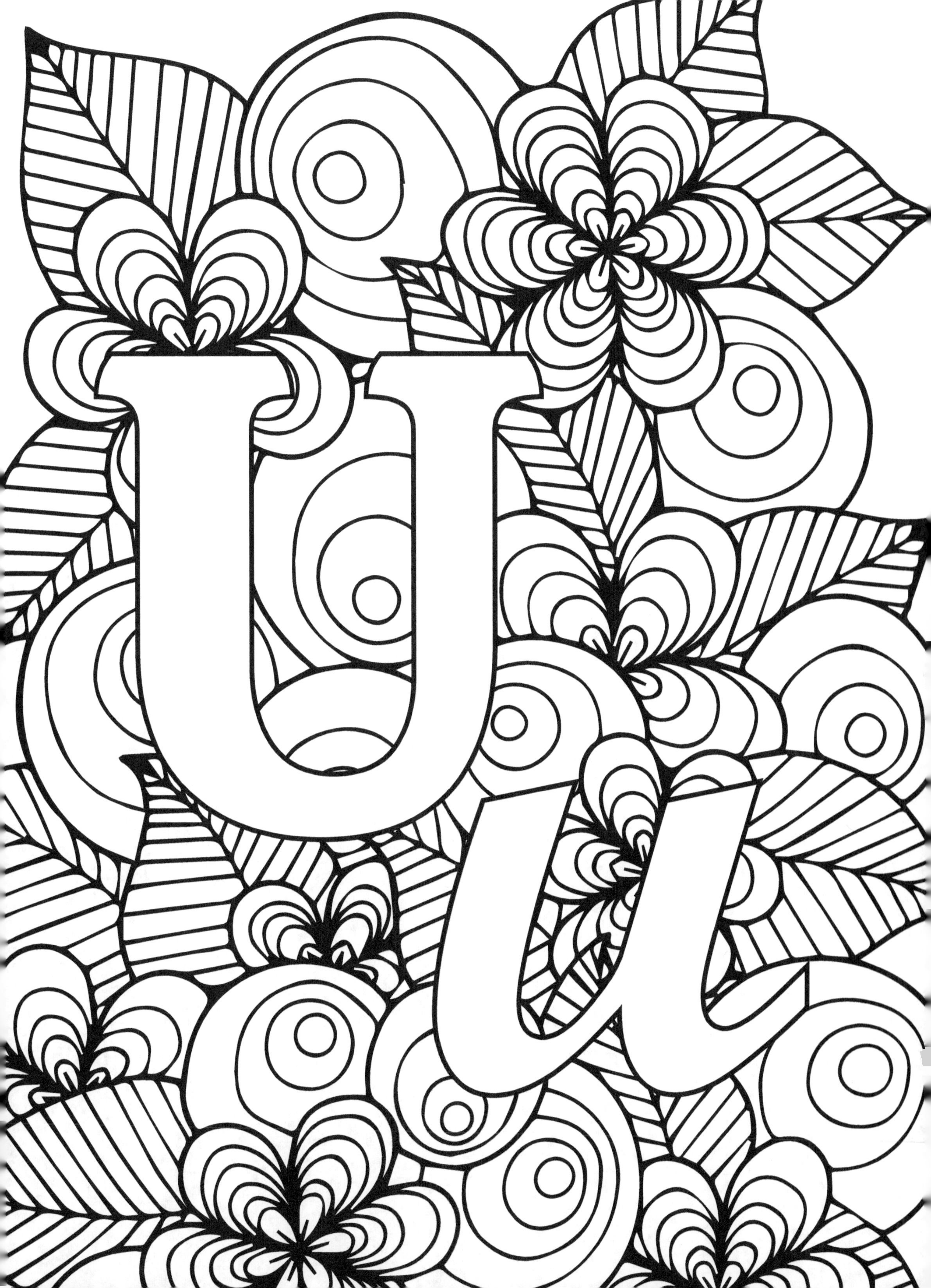

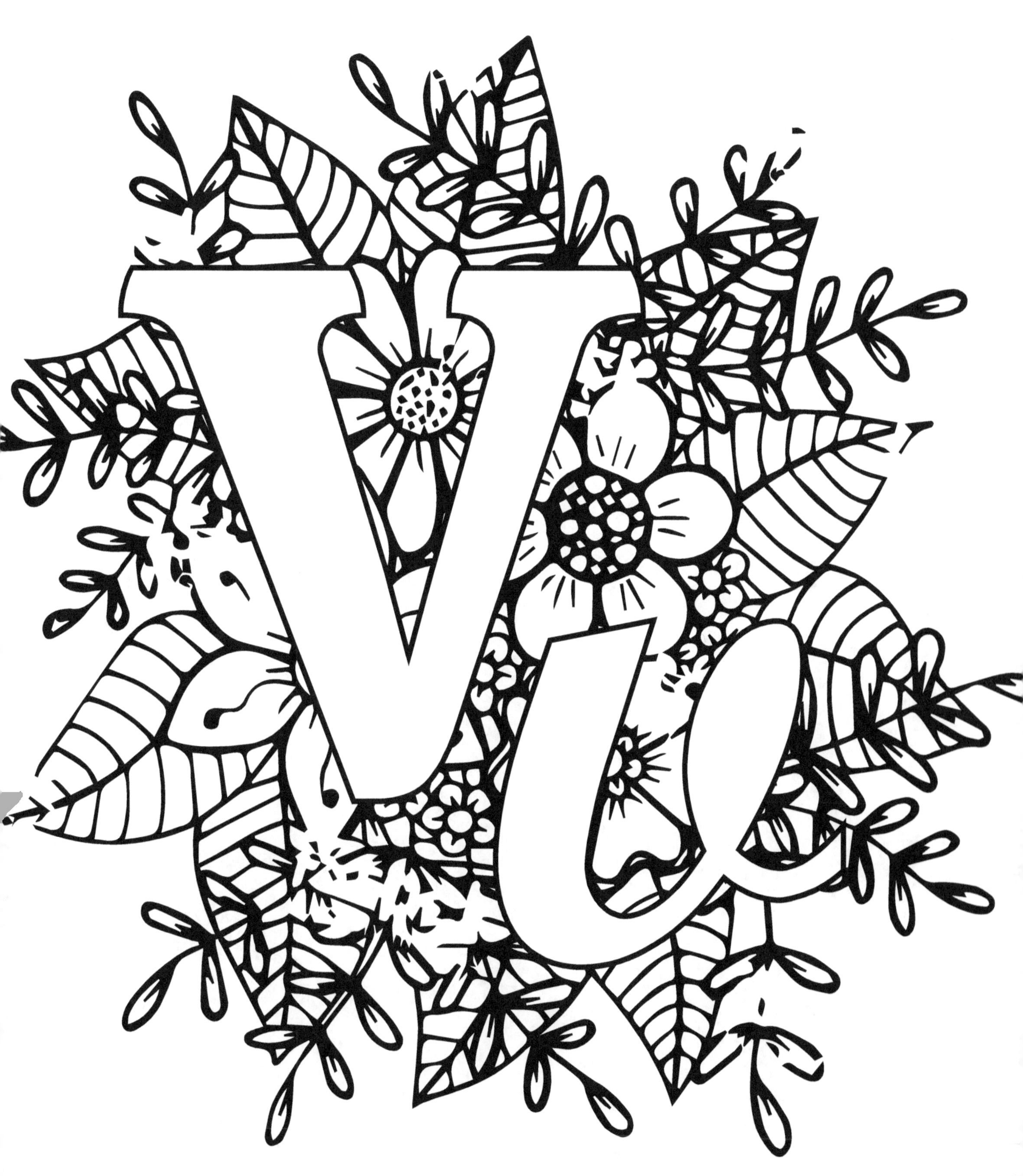

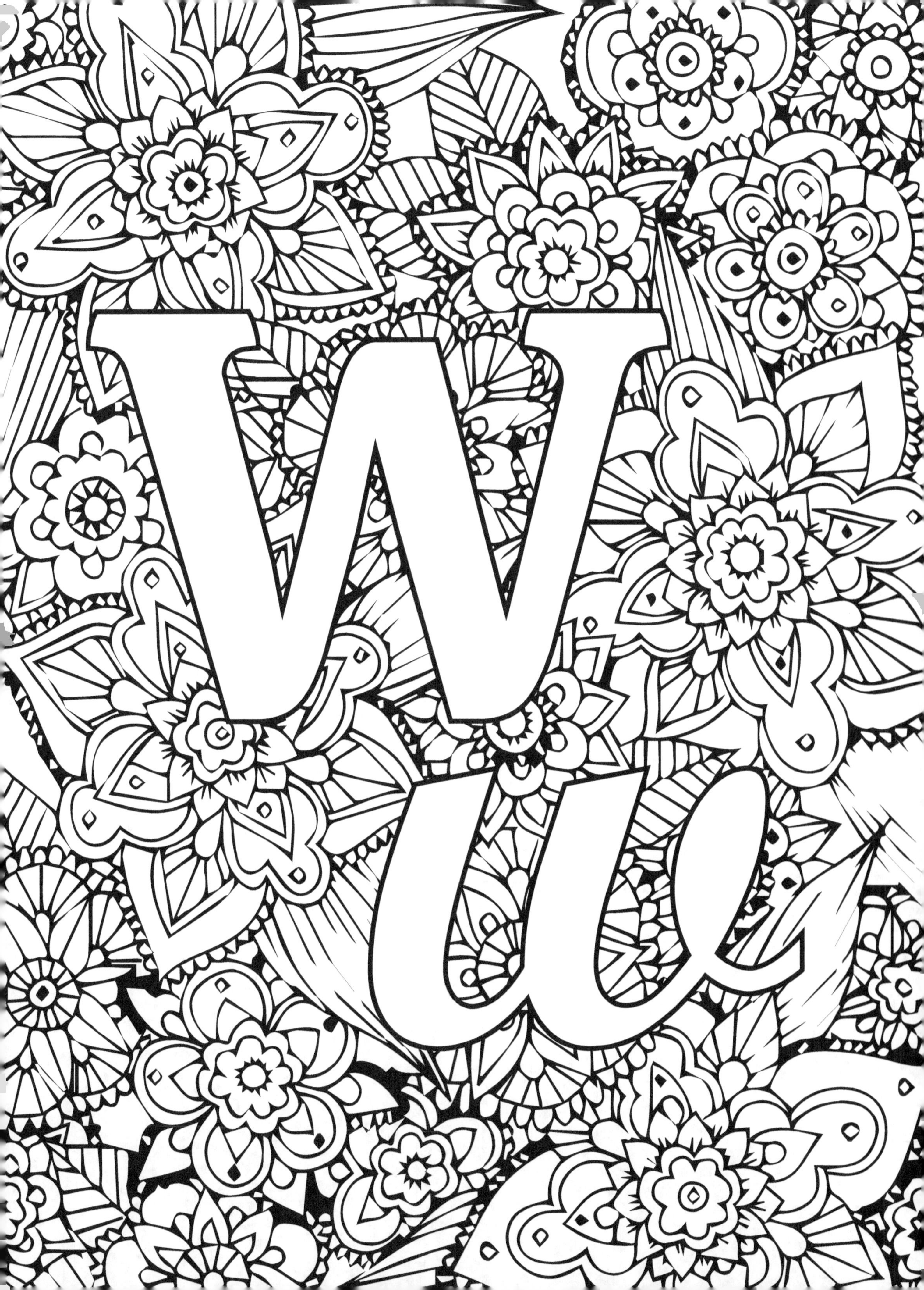

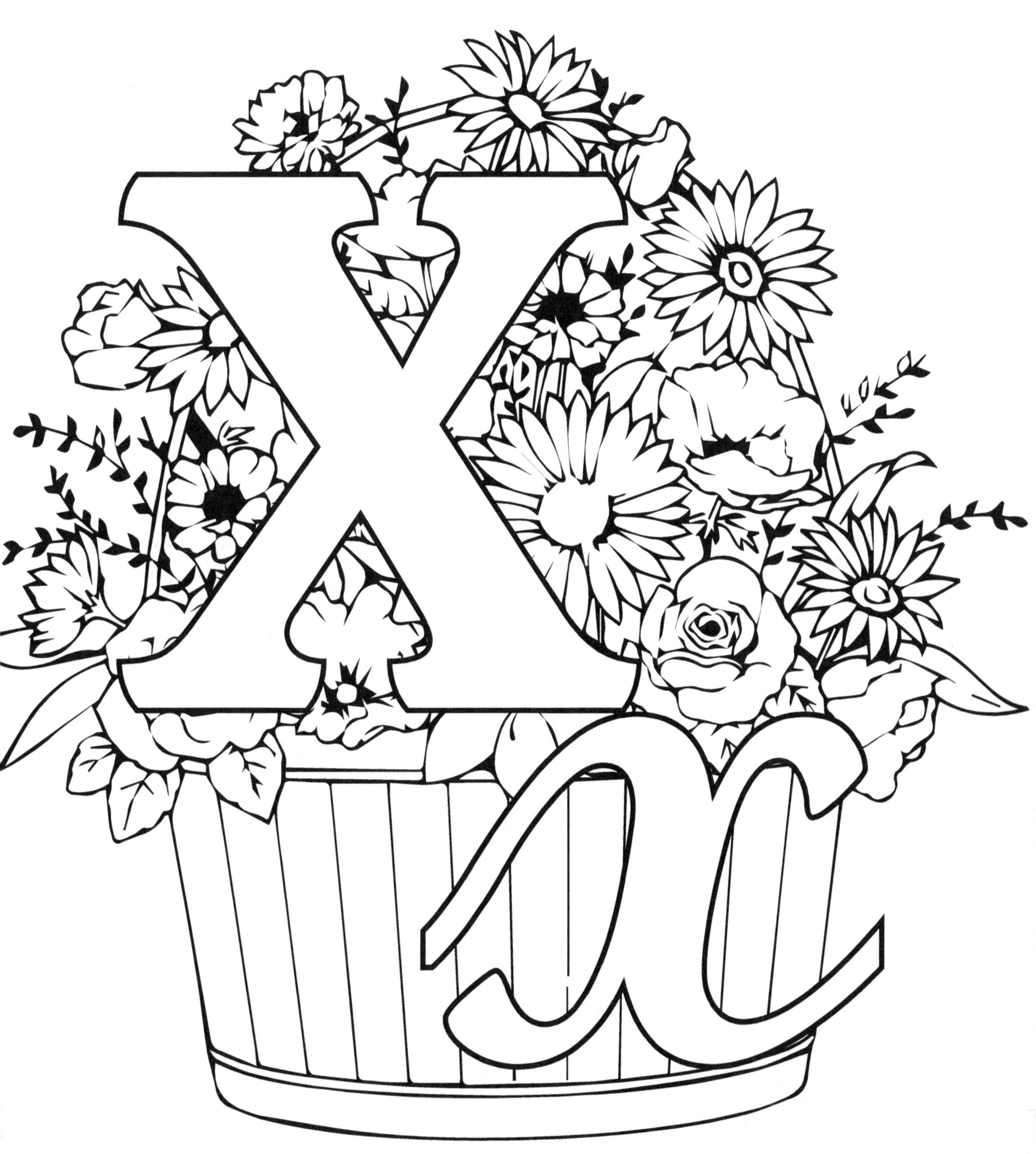

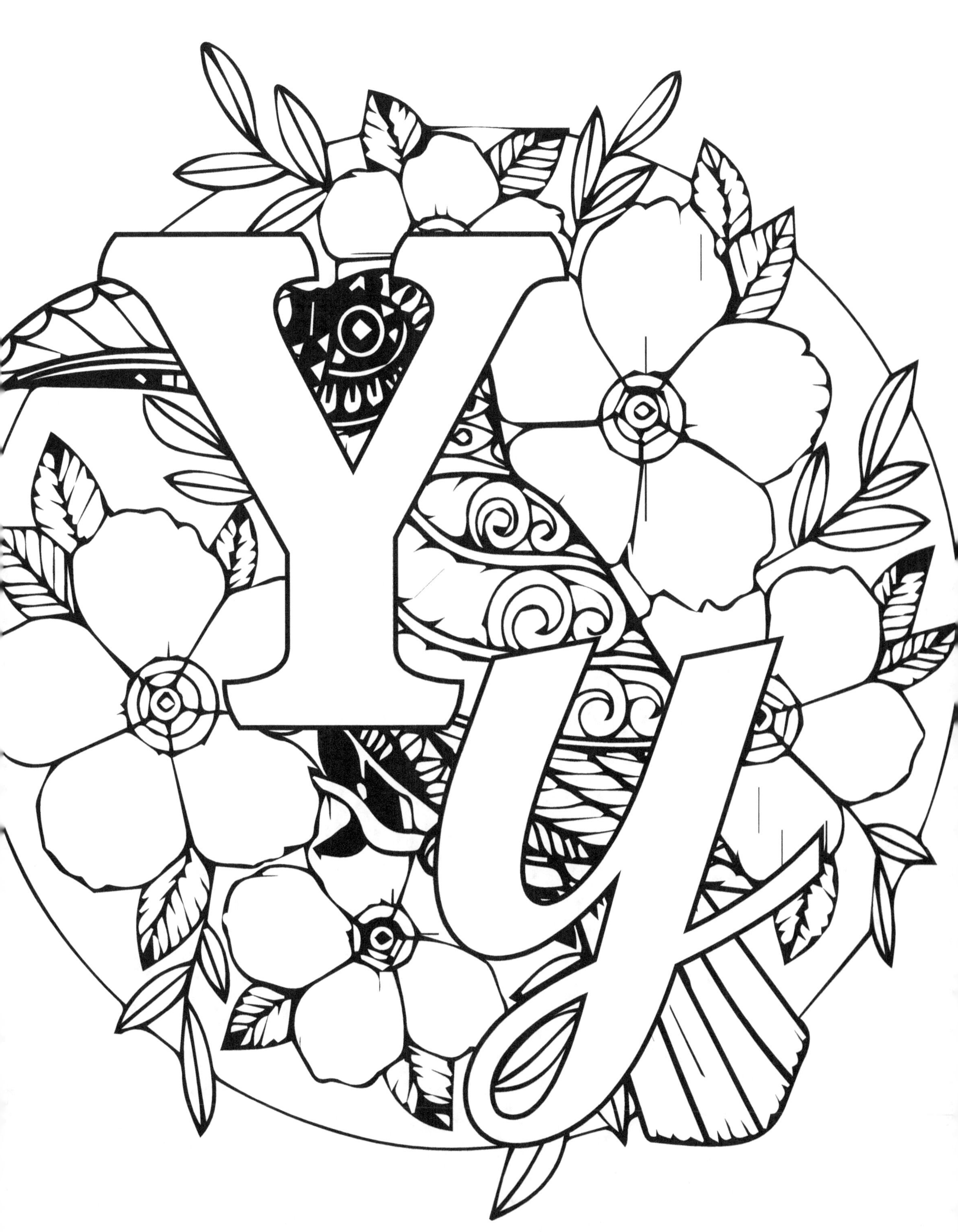

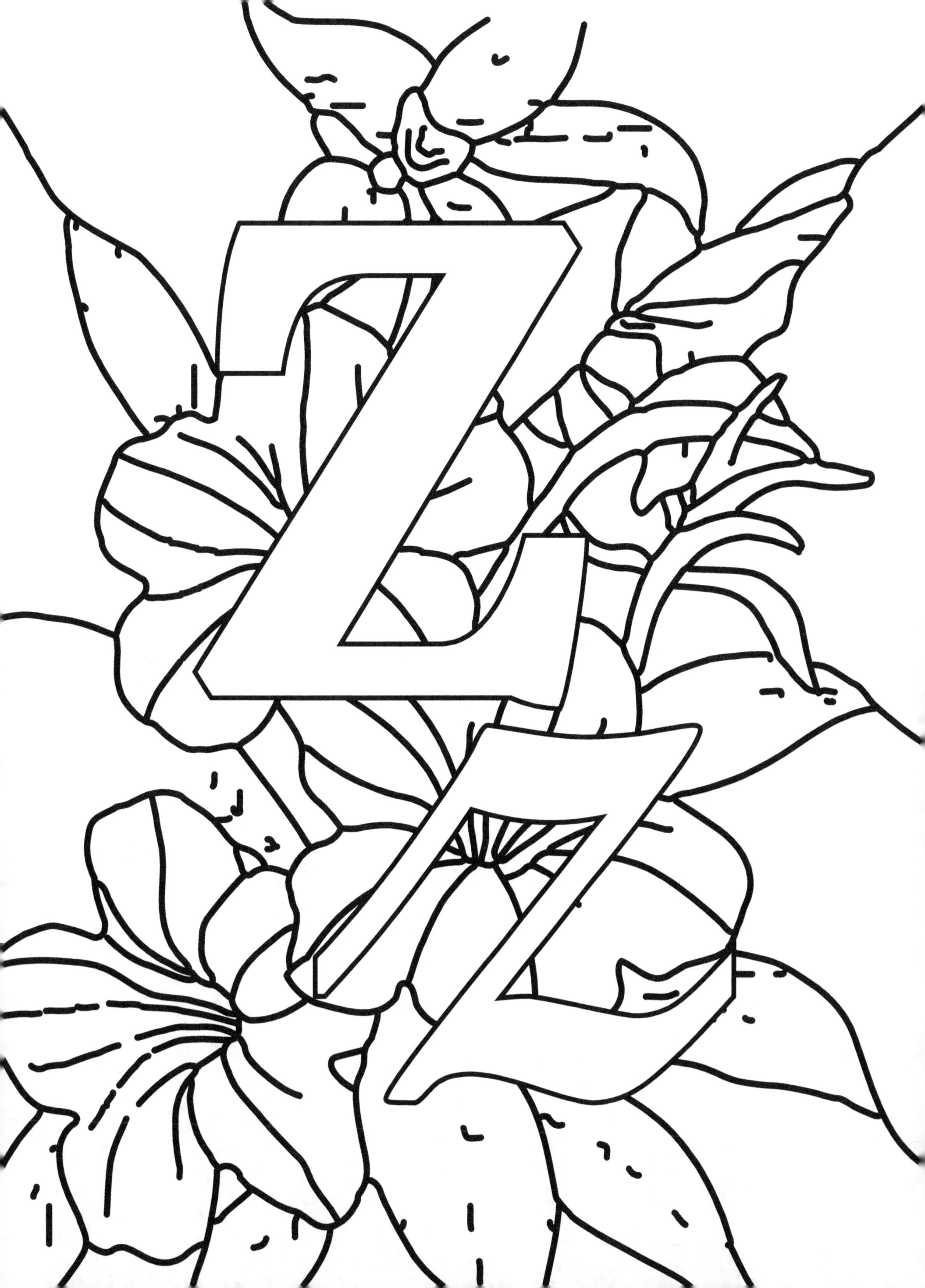

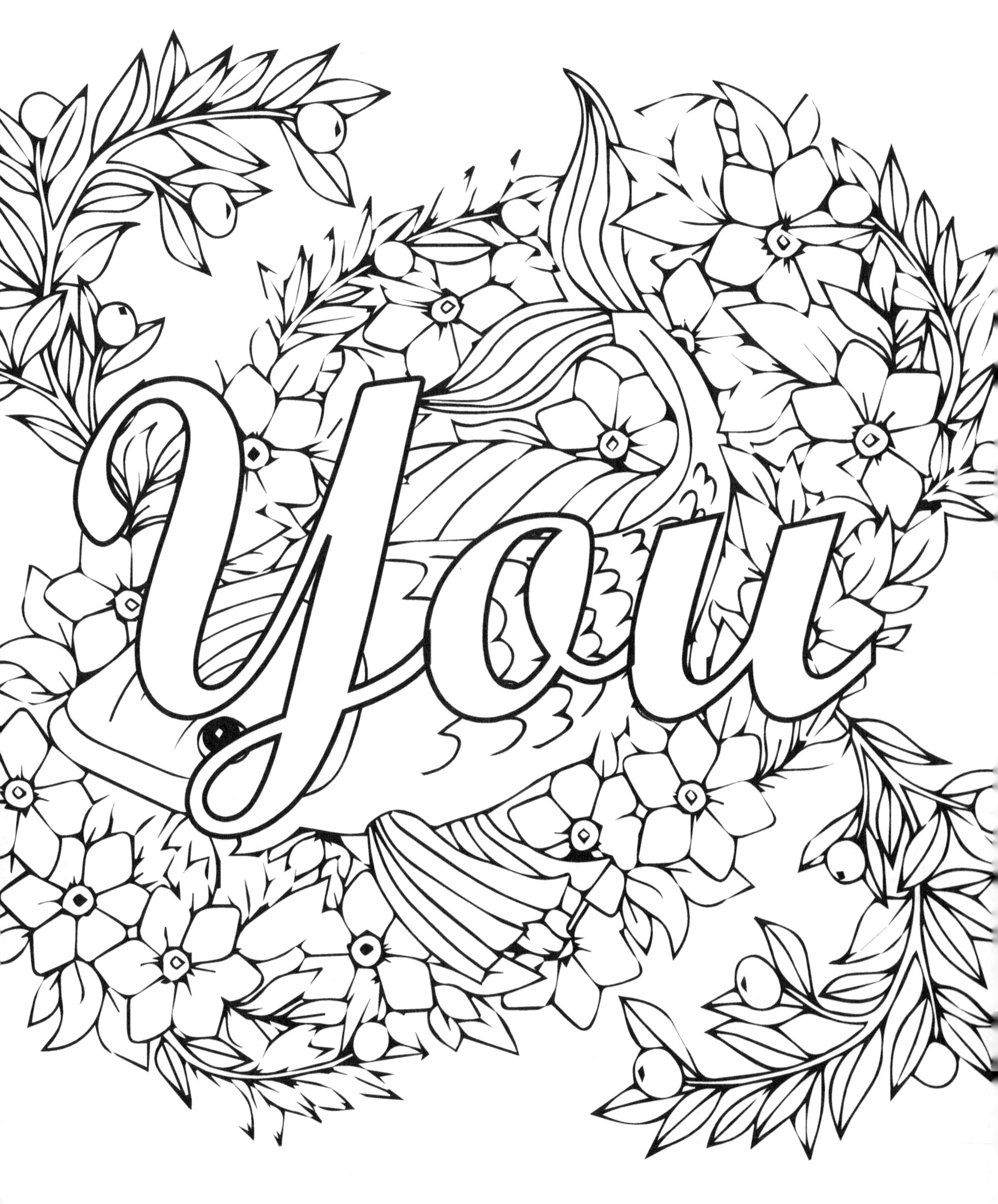

You

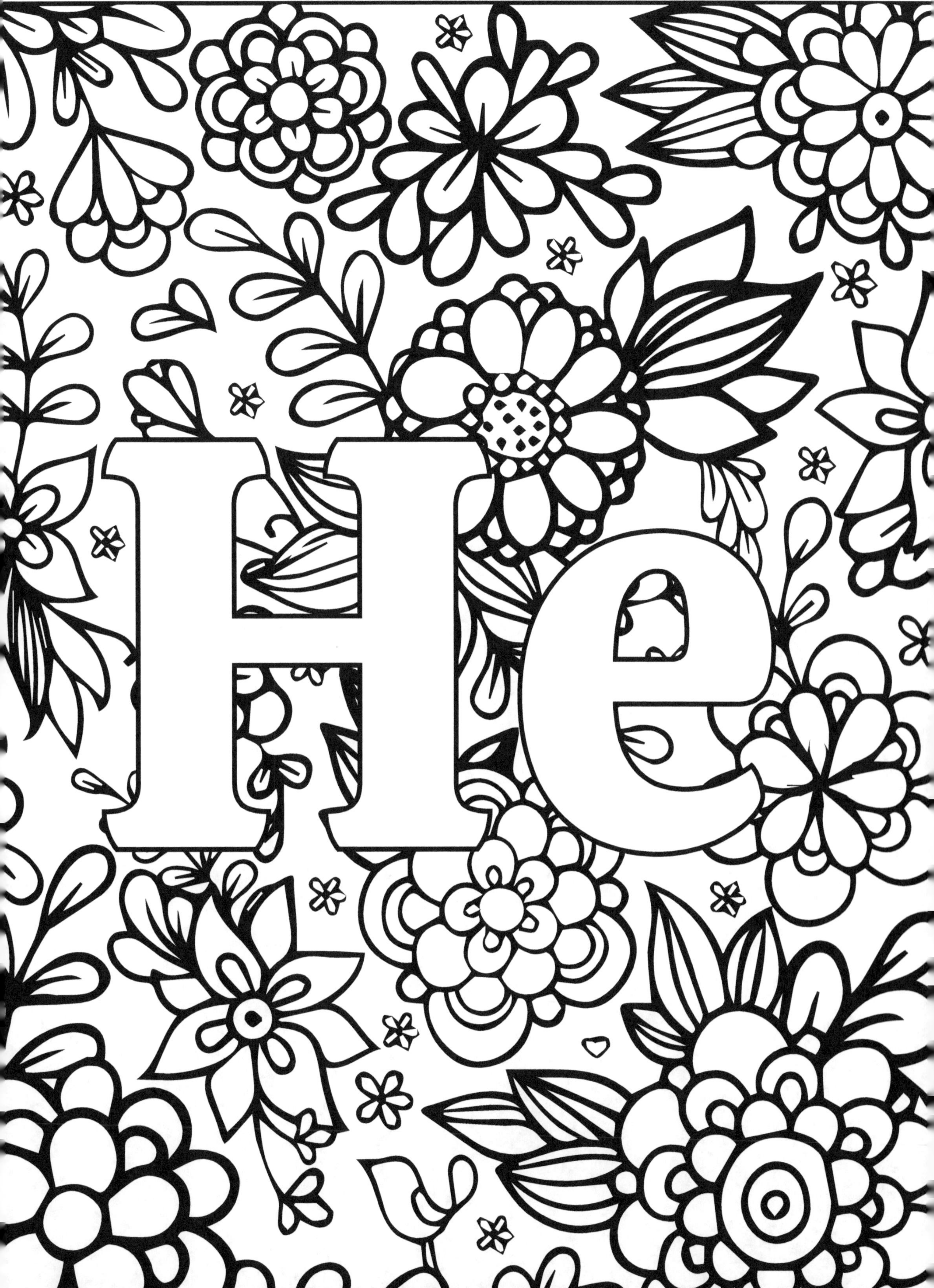

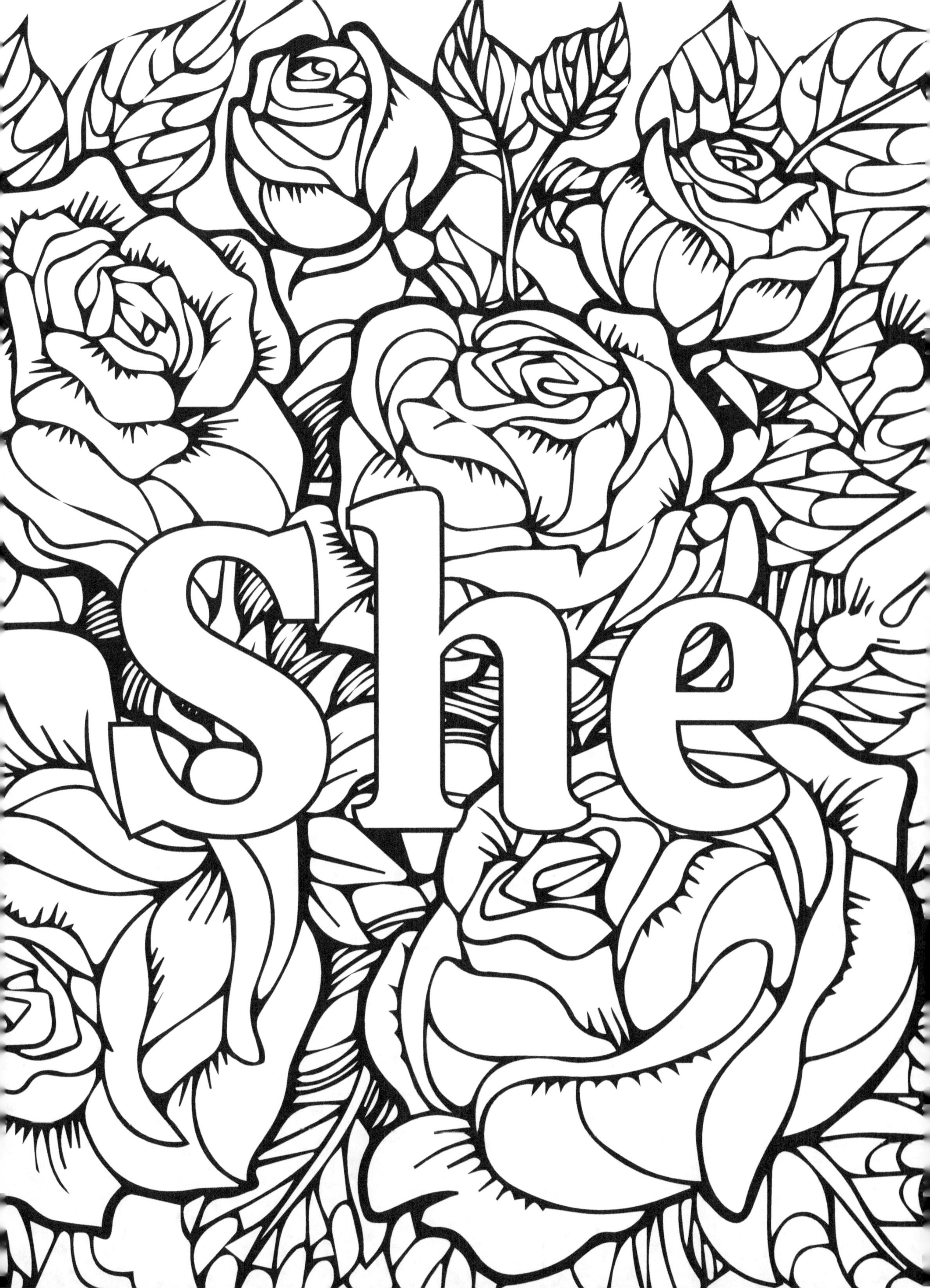

She

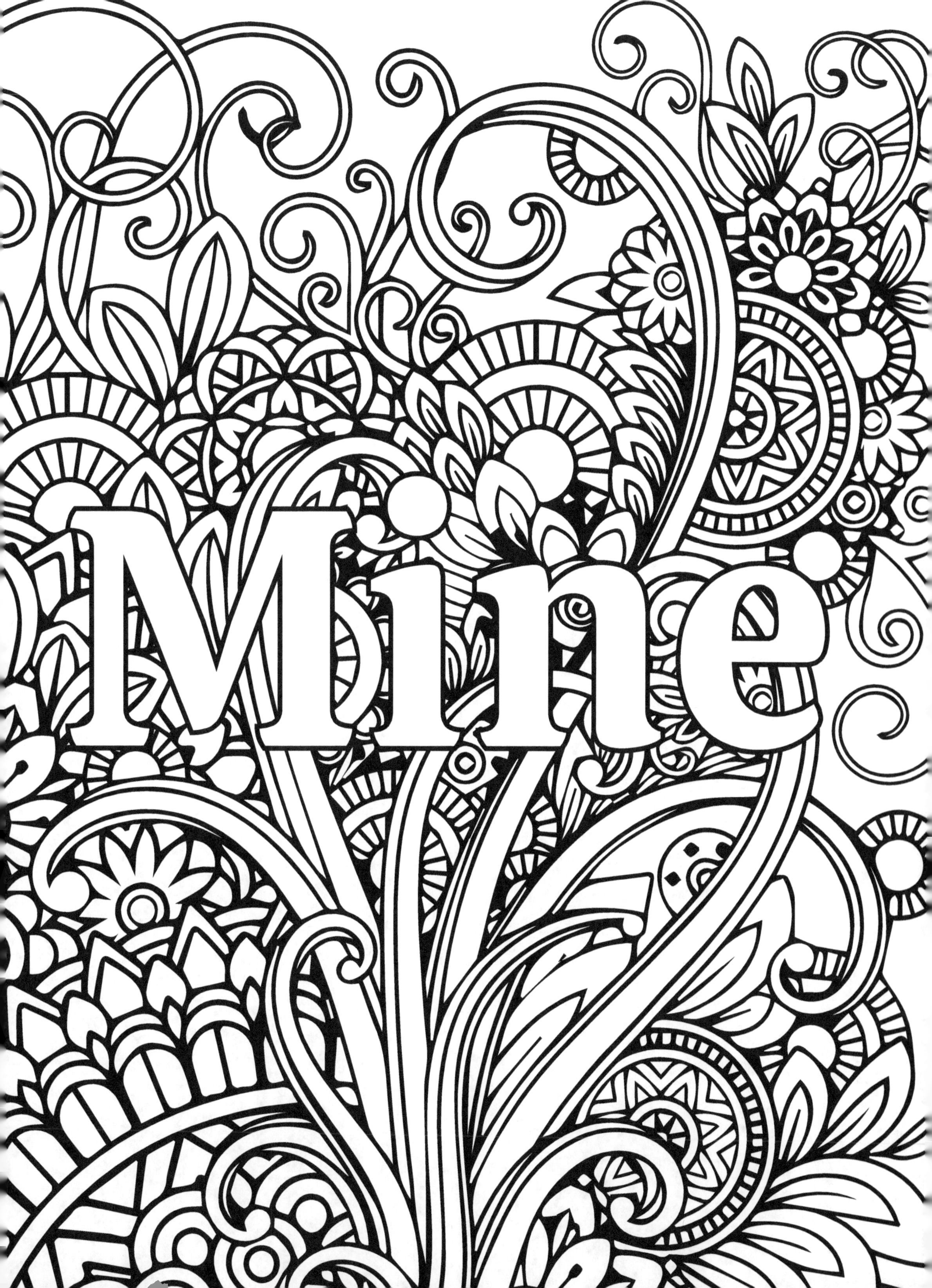
Mine

www.ingramcontent.com/pod-product-compliance
Lightning Source LLC
Chambersburg PA
CBHW080831260726
48654CB00027B/1858

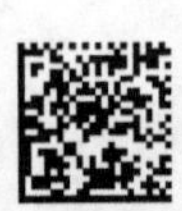